STUDENT EDI

JOHN

The Beloved Disciple

BETH MOORE

LifeWay Press
Nashville, Tennessee

Dewey Decimal Classification Number 225.92
Subject Heading: JOHN, APOSTLE \ BIBLE N.T.—STUDY \ DISCIPLESHIP TRAINING—YOUTH

This book is the text for course CG-0724 in the subject area "Personal Life"
in the Christian Growth Study Plan.

Unless otherwise noted, Scripture quotations are from the Holy Bible, *New International Version,*
copyright © 1973, 1978, 1984 by International Bible Society.

Printed in the United States of America.
To order additional copies of this resource: WRITE LifeWay Church Resources Customer Service,
One LifeWay Plaza, Nashville, TN 37234-0113; FAX orders to (615) 251-5933;
EMAIL to *CustomerService@lifeway.com;* ONLINE at *www.lifeway.com;*
or visit the LifeWay Christian Store serving you.

Art Direction and Designs: Edward Crawford

Student Ministry Publishing
LifeWay Christian Resources
of the Southern Baptist Convention
One LifeWay Plaza
Nashville, TN 37234-0174

CONTENTS

Meet Beth Moore

Beth Moore realized at the age of 18 that God was claiming her future for full-time ministry. While she was sponsoring a cabin of sixth graders at a missions camp, God unmistakably acknowledged that she would work for Him. There Beth gave all parts of her life to the Lord she had loved since childhood. However, she had a problem: although she knew she was "wonderfully made," she was fearfully without talent. She hid behind closed doors to discover whether a beautiful singing voice had miraculously developed, but the results were tragic. She returned to her piano from which years of practice resulted in joyless noise. Finally accepting that the only remaining alternative was missions work in a foreign country, she waited. Nothing happened.

Still confident of God's calling, Beth finished her degree at Southwest Texas State University, where she fell in love with Keith. After they married in December 1978, God added three blessings: Amanda, Melissa, and Michael.

As if putting together puzzle pieces one at a time, God filled Beth's path with supportive persons who saw something in her she could not. God used individuals like Marge Caldwell, John Bisagno, and Jeannette Cliff George to help Beth discover gifts of speaking, teaching, and writing. Now years after her first speaking engagement, those gifts have spread all over the world. Her joy and excitement in Christ are contagious; her deep love for the Savior, obvious; her style of speaking, electric.

Beth loves the Lord, loves to laugh, and loves to be with His people. Her life is full of activity, but one commitment remains constant: counting all things but loss for the excellence of knowing Christ Jesus, the Lord. (See Phil. 3:8.)

Introduction

The year was A.D. 28 … give or take a few. Those we will study together were Jews at a time when Judaism had perhaps never been more Jewish. By this expression I mean that although they were under Roman rule, they enjoyed very significant freedom to live out their culture. They were firmly established in their land and had their temple for worship.

The family was a powerful avenue through which God worked during this time. In those days, sons followed in their father's footsteps. Girls had no need of formal education. After all, they would simply grow up and do exactly as their mothers had done.

On the pebbles lining the northern shore of the Sea of Galilee, four little feet had earned their calluses. From the time they were knee high to their father, Zebedee, James and John tagged along after him as he went about the business of being a fisherman. He was responsible not only for making sure his rambunctious offspring didn't drown but also for harnessing their insatiable curiosity with his trade. He was their walking daycare center, and his sons' mother expected them home each day in one piece.

James held the coveted position in the family birth order. Special rights and privileges belonged to him as the firstborn. John? He was just the younger brother. John was a common name at the time, but the meaning was extraordinary: "God has been gracious."[1]

It was into this setting that suddenly the Word of God came through an unlikely vagabond also named John. (Read Matt. 3:1-6.) I wonder if all of heaven hushed to hear it. Of course, those on earth didn't have to hush. The Baptizer talked nice and loud. And when he was not nice, he was still loud. Loud enough, in fact, that Pharisees and Sadducees from Jerusalem went all the way to the Jordan to see what all the commotion was about. Theirs were among the few heads that stayed dry that day. They were not about to let this wild preacher baptize them.

"I am the voice of one calling in the desert, 'Make straight the way for the Lord.'"—John 1:23

So who was John the Baptist? Look at his own claim in John 1:23. I find what he said about himself very refreshing. He understood the greatness of Christ and how unworthy he was in comparison. His life had value through its connection to the Christ. John the Baptist introduced a concept that John the fisherman will carry on for us throughout our eight-week travel together. Among many other things, we're going to learn how to define ourselves by our relationship to Jesus Christ.

1. R. Alan Culpepper, *John, the Son of Zebedee* (Columbia, S.C.: University of South Carolina Press, 1994), 7.

Chapter One

A CALL TO FOLLOW

*Each of us is called into a relationship with Jesus,
to walk beside Him and become His disciple.*

KEY SCRIPTURE

WITHOUT DELAY HE
CALLED THEM, AND
THEY LEFT THEIR
FATHER ZEBEDEE IN
THE BOAT WITH THE
HIRED MEN AND
FOLLOWED HIM.
—MARK 1:20

John's Call to Follow

Passover was just around the corner. Spring had finally arrived and not a moment too soon for a band of fishermen who spent their days on the water. Winter temperatures ranging anywhere from 50 to 65 degrees Fahrenheit during the daytime may not have seemed so cold to landlovers; but fishermen would have told a different story. Sometimes their fingers would be so frigid they would temporarily lose their dexterity. Read Luke 5:1-5 for a little insight into a fisherman's life.

Obviously, the fishermen worked the graveyard shift at times. I can think of only one thing worse than fishing in the cold. Not catching anything. It happens to the best of fishermen. When it happens to my husband, Keith, I always ask him a typical woman question, "But did you have fun with your friends anyway?" My personality is given to the philosophy that the question is not so much whether you succeeded or failed, but did you have fun?

At the time Andrew, Peter, James, and John were casting their nets on the Sea of Galilee (also called Lake Gennesaret), a vigorous fishing industry was booming all over the lake. Many villages were settled on the shores of this freshwater lake. The Sea of Galilee boasts 18 species of fish, so fishing could have been profitable almost anywhere.

God wisely equipped us with four Gospels because we learn far more from hearing several accounts of anything especially noteworthy. The facts one person includes may not be noted by another because each point of view is tinted by the individual's perspective and priorities.

Read all accounts of Jesus' call to these four in the Scripture below and carefully record in the appropriate columns any facts unique to each Gospel.

Matthew 4:18-22　　　　　　　　　　**Mark 1:14-20**　　　　　　　　　**Luke 5:1-11**

REFLECTION

WAS THERE A POINT IN YOUR LIFE WHEN YOU SPECIFICALLY HEARD JESUS SAY TO YOU, "FOLLOW ME"; OR WERE YOU MORE AWARE OF HIS INVITATION OVER A SPAN OF YEARS?

I can go no further without musing over Christ's divinely uncanny ability to waltz right into a life and turn it upside down and inside out. Just think how many times those fishermen had cast their nets together. We would not be at all off base to imagine that they had caught fish since they were young boys, perhaps no older than seven or eight. I know you did not miss Luke's inclusion, "Master, we've worked hard all night and haven't caught anything." They worked hard. Day in. Day out. Then one day Jesus walked up, and everything changed.

Oh, Beloved, isn't that exactly like Him? Jesus walks right up, catches us in the act of being—again today—exactly who we were yesterday, and offers to turn our routine into adventure. Hallelujah! Have you allowed Christ to do that for you? Dear One, are you bored with life and stuck in a rut of routine? Have you believed in Christ but not yet agreed to follow Him? Christ is a lot of things, but boring? Not on your life! Life with Him is a great adventure. You don't necessarily have to leave behind what you are doing, but I assure you He will have you leave the boredom and routine of it behind.

When Jesus Christ takes over our lives, things get exciting! As we begin our journey together, plot where you feel you are presently.

●　·　·　·　·　·　○　·　·　·　·　·　○　·　·　·　·　·　○　·　·　·　·　·　○　·　·　·　·　·　○　·　·　·　·　·　○　·　·　·　·　·　●

Living routinely,　　　　　　　　　　　　　　　　　　　　　　　　　　**Living the**
in a rut　　　　　　　　　　　　　　　　　　　　　　　　　　　　　　**great adventure**

What name did Simon call Jesus in Luke 5:5?

__ Lord   __ Master   __ the Christ   __ Friend   __ Lamb of God

That's not the kind of title people use for a stranger unless they know the person is worthy of honor. I believe we can assume that these fishermen were familiar with this man called Jesus. Read the inclusions the Holy Spirit gave John in John 1:35-42.

Several of those who would become disciples of Jesus had been disciples of John the Baptist. Which do we know for certain based on this text?

__ Andrew   __ Peter   __ James   __ Matthew

Many scholars believe that John, the disciple whose life we will study, was the other of the two disciples mentioned in John 1:35. John as a rule did not identify himself in his writings. We know for certain Peter met Christ before his encounter with Him on the boat because John 1:42 tells us Andrew brought Peter to meet Jesus.

Without a doubt, Peter, Andrew, James, and John knew Christ at least by reputation based on John the Baptist's faithful ministry; and at least several of them knew Him by a prior encounter. When Jesus approached them at their boats, they were primed and readied by God to leave everything behind and follow Christ anywhere. I'd like to suggest that just as James and John were preparing their nets, they too had been prepared. The word *preparing* in Mark 1:19 can also mean "repairing." The exact same word is used in Galatians 6:1 for restoring a fallen brother. Oh, how thankful I am that the same God who prepares also repairs and restores.

At this season of your precious life, what do you sense you need most?
__ **Preparation for a fresh work of God**
__ **Repairing from a tear**
__ **Restoration from a kind of "fall"**

Write a few words of explanation below and a prayer in the margin.

I am reminded of a wonderful verse found in Joshua 3:5. "Consecrate yourselves, for tomorrow the Lord will do amazing things among you." God can perform a miracle in any one of us at any time, but amazing things happen when you and I are willing to get prepared for a mighty work of God.

No matter where you plotted yourself on the line on page 7, I pray that each of our testimonies at the conclusion of these eight weeks will cause us to need more room on the right margin. May our lives be off the scale with adventure!

🌴 On the Road with Jesus 🌴

Reread Mark 1:20. James and John left their father Zebedee in the boat with the hired men and followed Jesus. Chances are pretty good Zebedee thought their sudden departure was a phase and they'd get over it. Glory to God, they never did. Once we let Jesus Christ really get to us, we never get over Him.

"Come, follow me," Jesus said, "and I will make you fishers of men" (Mark 1:17). I love the fact that Jesus spoke in images His listeners could understand. When He said, "I will make you fishers of men," He obviously used terminology Andrew, Peter, James, and John could understand. He didn't use the same terminology with Philip, Nathanael, or Matthew; but I am convinced one part of the sentence applies to every single person Jesus Christ calls. He told them, "I will make you …."

Decades later when the disciples' lives had changed the face of religion forever, they still could not boast in themselves. Christ "made" them the men they were. I can't express what these thoughts mean to me. I was such a broken and scattered mess. So emotionally unhealthy. So insecure and full of fear. I am not falsely modest when I tell you that when Christ called me, He had pitifully little to work with. I was a wreck … and stayed that way for longer than I'd like to admit. I still have such a long way to go, but this I can say: Anything that I am or have of value is completely from Christ. He "made" me. You may have a similar testimony even at your young age.

So, how does Christ make a man or a woman? We can look at the lives of the disciples to see that He began building His new followers into the men He wanted them to be by spending intense time with them and showing them how He worked. I am convinced that we don't really know people until we stay with them for a few days. Can I hear an amen?

Take a look at Scriptures that describe Christ at this time in His ministry. For each reference, name the characteristic displayed by Jesus that would have attracted people to Him.
Mark 1:40-42

Luke 2:52

Luke 4:14-15

Luke 4:31-32

Do you see, Beloved? Christ was everything of any real value. He still is. People knew He was unique even before they knew He was God. Jesus had compassion. Favor. Wisdom. Power. Authority. He was the perfect man. Those who appreciated His uniqueness were drawn to it. Those who were threatened by it wanted Him destroyed.

The disciples saw Christ perform eye-opening miracles almost from the start. Please read Mark 1:21-28. Picture these four fishermen mingling in the crowd gathered that Sabbath in the synagogue in Capernaum. There was only one Jewish synagogue in the city, so they worshiped with

KEY SCRIPTURE

JESUS REPLIED, "LET US GO SOMEWHERE ELSE—TO THE NEARBY VILLAGES—SO I CAN PREACH THERE ALSO. THAT IS WHY I HAVE COME."—MARK 1:38

virtually the same people week after week. They knew them personally. There were relatives, neighbors, and business associates.

Talk about an interesting service! If an amazing message were not enough excitement, a man in their synagogue cried out. Suddenly all heads turned toward the opponent, almost like spectators in a tennis match. I wonder if the crowd previously knew this man had an evil spirit or if they had been oblivious for years to the nature of his problems.

Picture John witnessing these events. Many scholars believe John was the youngest of the disciples. If he was, can you imagine his face while Jesus encountered—then cast out—this demon? John probably experienced an entire concoction of emotions. Young men dearly love competitions, so he had to savor seeing his new team "win" even if only one Player was involved in the match. I have to think the encounter also scared him half to death. One thing that might have offset his fear was that he had to be indescribably impressed with his new mentor. But he wasn't the only one. Mark 1:22 tells us the crowds were amazed by Christ's teachings.

I have a feeling that by the time the fishermen reached Capernaum with Jesus, so did the news of their leaving Zebedee holding the net. I don't doubt for a minute that these young men whose reputations were on the line reveled in the grand reaction people in the community had to their new Leader. The day was far from over. Read what happened next in Mark 1:29-34.

Most likely, the first healing of the sick ever witnessed by the disciples was in Simon Peter's home. Surely an early turning point came in the hearts and minds of the disciples when healing hit home. I know it did for me. Seeing Him work in a church service is one thing. Witnessing His healing in the life of your own family is another. That's when a person begins to get it through his or her head that Jesus doesn't just love church. He loves people.

Compare Mark 1:21 and 29. When did this healing occur?
__ on the Sabbath   __ during Passover   __ on the Lord's day

Christ angered the Pharisees on several occasions by picking this particular day for healing, as if He were making a point. Obviously, Christ saw the purpose of the day far differently than many of His contemporaries. Apparently Simon Peter's mother was healed just in time to rise from the bed and get ready for company.

What happened literally at her front door after sunset? (See Mark 1:32-34.)

Few of us choose to confront suffering because we feel so helpless. Imagine the contrast between the agony of seeing human suffering and the ecstasy of seeing people healed. What would such an experience have been like for John? John was a human being, just like you. Possibly, the same age as you. Let's imagine how these sights affected him.

John had observed hundreds of Sabbaths in his life. Imagine that he awakened that morning in Capernaum thinking, "I can hardly believe what I've done! I wonder what my mom and dad are thinking right now." He's excited and unsure, and his soul is filled with the reality that something new is looming on the horizon. He prepares to go to the synagogue for services just as he has done all his life, only this time he gets a bit more than he bargained for. The scroll is opened, and the Scripture for the day's service is read. Then Jesus takes the role of rabbi, sits down, and preaches the locks nearly off their heads!

Just then a man possessed by a demon starts shouting, and John sees Jesus get stern ... perhaps for the first time. In an astounding show of power, Jesus casts out the demon, causing the man to shake violently. As long as he lives, John feels like he'll never forget the sound of the demon shrieking. He and the other disciples walk together to Simon Peter's house, whispering all the way about what they've seen. Simon Peter's mother-in-law is sick with a fever, so Jesus takes her by the hand and helps her up; and the fever leaves her so instantaneously she begins to serve them.

Then they begin to hear sounds at the door. Murmurings. Shrieking. Crying. Sounds of moaning. Sounds of hope. What's that? Hope? Yes, hope. And hope says, "What He did for her, He might do for me." Imagine being John. Imagine all he had seen during the course of the day.

I can only imagine the kinds of things that went through the mind of the young disciple. He probably tossed and turned most of the night. Perhaps he and James whispered to each other from their pallets until they were overtaken by exhaustion and finally fell asleep. As I imagine all that had happened that Saturday and all they had seen, I know one of the thoughts I would have had if I had been John. *Is there anything the man can't do?* He watched Jesus practically bring the house down with His teaching. He watched Him confront and cast out a demon from a man that came to synagogue. He watched Him heal Simon's mother-in-law and instantly restore her strength. Then every manner of distress landed on the doorstep.

I love Matthew Henry's words of commentary on the scene at the door: "How powerful the Physician was; he healed all that were brought to him, though ever so many. Nor was it some one particular disease, that Christ set up for the cure of, but he healed those that were sick of divers [various, diverse] diseases, for his word was a panpharmacon—a salve for every sore."[1]

His Word was a panpharmacon, a salve for every sore. Ah, yes. I have yet to have an ailment God had no salve to soothe. But what may be even more peculiar is that I have yet to have an ailment of soul that God's Word was not the first to point out, diagnose, then heal. His Word is far more glorious, powerful, and fully applicable than we have any idea. Read Psalm 107:20.

How often God had to send forth His Word and begin His spiritual healing. Every time God has prepared us with His Word and gotten us to a point that we could receive a hard "pill" to swallow from Him, spiritual healing had already begun. He doesn't always heal physical ailments; His healing always begins in the heart. Take heart. He is the Panpharmacon.

REFLECTION

IF YOU WERE JOHN, WHAT PART OF THE DAY WOULD YOU THINK ABOUT THE MOST? WHY?

He sent forth his word and healed them. —Psalm 107:20

🦂 A Solitary Place 🦂

KEY SCRIPTURE

**VERY EARLY IN THE MORNING, WHILE IT WAS STILL DARK, JESUS GOT UP, LEFT THE HOUSE AND WENT OFF TO A SOLITARY PLACE, WHERE HE PRAYED. SIMON AND HIS COMPANIONS WENT TO LOOK FOR HIM.
—MARK 1:35-36**

Jesus looked up and said, "Father, I thank you that you have heard me. I knew that you always hear me." —John 11:41-42

After the kind of day Jesus had on Saturday, if I had been Him, I might have considered sleeping in. Not Jesus. While the disciples may have whispered from their makeshift beds about all they had seen, the One with whom Jesus longed to speak wasn't on the next pallet. While it was still dark, Jesus got up, left the house, and went off to a solitary place, where He prayed. He slipped out of the house that morning after the Sabbath because He had a private Sunday morning service to attend. The wood placard that hung on the wall right above the organist at my first church would have read: Today's Attendance: 2.

In Matthew 6:6, Christ taught: "But when you pray, go into your room, close the door and pray to your Father." Where is your favorite place to pray? What makes that place work for you?

Jesus went to a private place for one reason: to be alone with His Father. Oh, how I would love to know how He prayed! What He said! How long He talked! Christ's prayers from planet earth were unique. He had a freedom and familiarity that others cloaked in human flesh could not comprehend. Surely that's one reason why the disciples pleaded with Him at a different time, "Lord, teach us to pray" (Luke 11:1). Hebrew men were taught to pray from the time they could speak. They recited specific prayers off and on all day long. They knew how to pray as men taught to pray; but when they beheld Christ captivated by the presence of His Father for hours at a time, I believe they meant, "Teach us to pray like that!"

I think John 11:41-42 indicates why Christ was so drawn to prayer and could pray for hours. He was convinced of two critical factors: (1) that His Father was the Omnipotent Creator and Sustainer of the universe, and (2) that the Father always heard His prayers. Do we not find our minds wandering and ourselves even a tad bored in prayer at times because we wonder if our words are bouncing off the ceiling? How differently would we pray if Christ sat in a chair right across from each of us, leaning forward to concentrate on what we're saying?

Beloved, though He's invisible to our sight, that is in essence what He does! He intercedes for us at the right hand of the Father. When we pray, He is so close to us that He may as well be leaning over the edge of heaven and bending down to hear from earth. His Presence through His Holy Spirit literally surrounds you as you pray. His eyes are fixed on your face. On every word you're saying. On every expression you're making. Can you imagine how the angels marvel over our boredom at times when we pray as their faces behold our Father in heaven who is listening intently to every word?

I want to give you a personal prayer assignment this week for you to practice and then discuss in your small group. Every time you pray for the next week, begin your prayer with "I know You always hear me." Then conclude it with "Father, I thank You that You have heard me." Practice God's presence! Pray like He's really listening because He is!

In our scene in Mark 1:35-37, the disciples were far too immature in their walk with Christ to consider the enormity of the scene they walked upon. Instead, they blurted out, "Everyone is looking for you!" Ah, here we have an insight into their present state of mind. Forget what Jesus did in private! They wanted to be seen in public with the popular Jesus! We're not going to be too hard on them because they were demonstrating a normal part of immature Christianity. We are the same way in our spiritual immaturity. At first we are far more excited about corporate worship than we are private worship, because we frankly don't know Him well enough to have as much to say one-to-One. We love the excitement of being in the masses of those who are enthralled by Christ, and we always will. However, as we mature and Jesus becomes a greater personal reality to us, I think we come to treasure time in the solitary places with Him more than anything.

Mark 1:36 tells us that Simon Peter and his companions went to look for Jesus. John was most likely among them. Notice they weren't called disciples yet. I'm not sure they qualified as learners yet! Whoever the companions were, the original language tells us they were tracking Jesus down, almost like a manhunt. They appeared to be quite anxious and maybe even a little "put out" with Him. We see no indication from the text that they hesitated for a moment out of respect or awe when they found Jesus praying. They barreled upon the scene with, "Everyone is looking for you!"

I would like to offer a little conjecture that the companions tracking down Jesus may have been Peter, James, and John. Later in His ministry, Christ chose three men—Peter, James, and John—to watch Him on different occasions in the "inner places." Something caused Jesus to single them out. I believe Scripture will prove that it wasn't their spiritual maturity. I think two primary motivations compelled Christ to draw the three into several intimate places: (1) The fact that they just didn't "get it" at times. (2) The fact that Jesus knew once they did "get it," they'd really get it! In other words, I wonder if Christ might have thought, *So you're not the boundaries types, are you? OK, I'll take you behind some ordinary boundaries; but I'll hold you responsible for what you learn while you're there.*

My friend's little boy thought he was the teacher's pet because she seated him in class right in front of her desk. He didn't realize for years that she was motivated by his discipline problems. Why didn't she just send him to the principal? Because she knew the child had a student in him, and she was determined to find it. And that she did.

Over the next two weeks, we're going to see Peter, James, and John get their desks moved to the front of the class. And just like children, at times they might be tempted to think the Rabbi moved them there because they were the Teacher's pets.

REFLECTION

DO YOU HAVE A PARTICULAR PLACE WHERE YOU ENCOUNTER GOD EACH DAY THROUGH PRAYER AND SCRIPTURE READING? IF NOT, START TODAY. SET ASIDE A TIME AND PLACE WHERE YOU WILL PRAY AND READ SCRIPTURE DAILY.

The Inner Circle

KEY SCRIPTURE

AFTER SIX DAYS JESUS TOOK PETER, JAMES AND JOHN WITH HIM AND LED THEM UP A HIGH MOUNTAIN, WHERE THEY WERE ALL ALONE. —MARK 9:2

REFLECTION

HAS A DEATH LEFT YOU WITH UNFINISHED BUSINESS? FINISH IT WITH JESUS.

Although I wish we could go through every step the disciples took with Christ, the purpose of this eight-week journey is to draw riches from the life and letters of the apostle John. This week, we're looking through the Synoptic (first three) Gospels and concentrating on the settings where John is named or known to be present. Today we're going to look at two scenes with some common denominators that no doubt profoundly affected young John.

Scene One: Mark 5:22-23,35-43
Read this passage. Pretend you are John and you keep a journal. What entry would you have made that evening before you fell asleep?

You and I most likely noted several of the same things. Perhaps the most noteworthy one for our present purposes is that Jesus singled out Peter, James, and John to accompany Him.

I have no idea what went through the minds of the three men when they were allowed to follow Jesus to a place the others weren't invited, but I know what would have gone through my feminine mind. I would hardly have been able to enjoy the privilege without fretting over the others being left out. I would then have worried about whether they would be mad at me when we got back. I would imagine for days that they were acting a little weird. In fact, knowing I would have fretted myself half to death, Jesus wouldn't have bothered letting me come. No telling how many things I've missed because I make a knot out of the simplest string!

I would have hated to miss the eyeful the three got that particular day. Raising the stone-cold dead is nothing less than divine. This scene was not business-as-usual no matter how many miracles the three had seen.

Look back at Mark 5:35. The death of a loved one is no time to quit "bothering" Jesus. Although He's not very likely to raise our loved ones from the dead, He can do countless other things to get us through our grief. Comfort is the most obvious need.

Scene Two: Mark 9:2-10
Much time lapsed between the two scenes we're studying today. Significant events occurred between these two dates, like the feeding of the five thousand and Jesus walking on the water. What makes these two scenes priorities for our study is the inclusion of only three disciples. Christ does nothing haphazardly. He undoubtedly had reasons for inviting their observation. In Mark 5:37, the three were listed as Peter, James, and John the brother of James. In this scene, John is no longer named like a tag-along brother. At this point, we see his identity in Scripture undoubtedly emerging. Also note that Jesus didn't just let Peter, James, and John come along. He took them.

Just as Jesus was intentional toward the experiences of these three disciples, He is intentional toward us. He never bosses us or appoints us to something for the sheer sake of assuming authority. His will always has purpose. Sometimes we go our own ways and God still has mercy on us and shows us something there. Other times we beg Him to allow us to go a certain place, and He consents. Still other times God takes us places we never intended to go. Those are places where He will reveal Himself to us in ways we didn't even know existed.

This scene is recorded in all three Synoptic Gospels. Each supplies a bit of unique information. Compare them and note in the proper column below each unique piece of information.

Matthew 17:1-9   Mark 9:2-10   Luke 9:28-36

Don't be alarmed by the difference in the time segments. "After six days" and "about eight days" can easily be figured into the same period of time because the Jews often counted any portion of a day as an additional day. Luke's word "about" relieves us of any concern regarding contradiction. Can you even imagine what the three disciples beheld?

Matthew's Gospel tells us that the three disciples fell facedown to the ground. I am convinced that the people of God miss many appropriate opportunities to fall facedown to the ground, not in an emotional frenzy, but in complete awe of God. We don't have a clue who we're dealing with. I believe one of Jesus' chief reasons for transfiguring Himself before the three disciples was to say, "I am not like you. This is just a glimpse of who I am." Remember, He had equipped them with supernatural power to perform some of the same miracles He performed. What would keep them from thinking just maybe in time they might be His peer? God forbid the thought! Jesus is not a super-human. He is God. One primary reason He takes us places we've never been is to show us He's not like anyone else.

Glory came down on the mountain that day. When the cloudy pillar enveloped them and the voice of the Almighty became audible, they clung to the dirt of earth in terror. Rightly so.

Mark's Gospel shares two additional facts. First of all, he tells us Christ's clothes dazzled with a whiteness whiter than any bleach could bleach them. You and I can't fathom whiter than white. Our finite minds can only embrace earth's own rendition of white … fresh-fallen snow on a bright, sunny day.

Mark also tells us that Peter made the daft suggestion of building three tents because he did not know what to say. He was frightened. Have you ever noticed how often we say something completely ridiculous when we don't know what to say? In God's wisdom He gave us twice as many ears as we have mouths, but we seem to miss the point all too often. God responded from the heavens, "This is My Son, whom I love. Listen to Him!" My translation: "Shut thee up!"

One of Luke's primary inclusions is the fact that Moses and Elijah were there discussing Christ's departure. A more literal translation would be "exodus." That puts chills all over me. If any two former mortals knew anything about distinctive departures, Moses and Elijah did. One died alone with God and was buried by Him, and the other was taken up in a whirlwind with chariots of fire. Jesus' departure would be more radical, and the effects would be completely revolutionary. They had much to discuss.

We've studied two scenes today. Both involved profound miracles. Both involved Christ's power over the dead. Jairus' daughter was raised from the dead. Neither Moses nor Elijah were returned back to their mortal bodies on earth, yet they were very much alive. In fact, Luke describes them in glorious splendor.

Jesus let the three disciples follow Him to Jairus' house and took them up the mountain to see Him transfigured. What points do you think He was trying to make to Peter, James, and John? What point do you think Jesus is trying to make to you today?

Beloved, Jesus is Lord over the living … and the dead.

KEY SCRIPTURE

THEY REPLIED, "LET ONE OF US SIT AT YOUR RIGHT AND THE OTHER AT YOUR LEFT IN YOUR GLORY." —MARK 10:37

To keep me from becoming conceited because of these surpassingly great revelations, there was given me a thorn in my flesh, a messenger of Satan, to torment me. —2 Corinthians 12:7

Misunderstanding Authority

Our reactions to God's revelation are tell-tale signs of our maturity. Even the most mature believers can be enticed by the enemy (Satan) and their own egos puffed up by God's revelation. Paul said it best in 2 Corinthians 12:7.

What is the obvious risk of great revelation, and how did God safeguard Paul against it?

Somebody might have needed to stick a thorn in Peter, James, and John as well and burst their ballooning egos. Did you notice in our previous lesson that the three didn't fall facedown on the ground until God spoke from the cloud? (See Matt. 17:5-6.) Can you imagine still being able to stand on your feet and talk while Christ dazzled with glory and Elijah and Moses popped onto the scene? Nope, the three weren't thinking very clearly. Sometimes we don't when our heads are too heady.

The three didn't exactly react with maturity. In the same chapter recording Christ's transfiguration, Luke reports two scenes. Identify the attitude of the disciple(s) in each passage.
Luke 9:46-48

Luke 9:49-50

Luke 9:51-55

Sometimes I wonder why God doesn't give up on us when we cop attitudes like pride and exclusivity. Only His mercy keeps us from being consumed. (See Lam. 3:22.) I constantly thank Him for hanging in there with me. I would have given up on myself a long time ago. I am so grateful that God sees us not only as we really are but also as how we will really become.

Perhaps John's age didn't help. Life simply hadn't had time to beat him over the head with humility. Forty years on the far side of the desert followed by a flock of aggravating people was enough to humble the exclusivity right out of Moses.

After the three strikes recorded in Luke 9, Christ's enduring love and patience is obvious in His unwillingness to throw His thumb back and yell "Out!" Particularly since He knew what was coming next. Take a good look at Mark 10:35-45.

Didn't James and John sum up the approach of spiritual toddlers? "We want you to do whatever we ask."

Can you relate? Write one way you support the same philosophy.

We can relate too much to want to judge James and John harshly in their approach, can't we? Let's face it. All of us have to go through spiritual toddlerhood and adolescence to get to a place of maturity. We don't ordinarily leap up. We grow up. The danger is when we refuse to grow. To get stuck in this stage is about as appealing as an adult who still acts like a two year old.

For a few moments, James and John do nothing but descend deeper and deeper in the quicksand of their own self-absorption. In this scene, James and John make only three statements.
• "Teacher, we want You to do for us whatever we ask."
• "Let one of us sit at Your right and the other at Your left in Your glory."
• "We can."

Think for a moment about the emotions and attitudes behind these statements. Do you see a growing audacity with each statement? Don't think for a minute they wouldn't have dug themselves deeper given the opportunity. Had Christ told them He might consider one on His right and one on His left, how long do you think it would have taken them to rumble over who would sit where? Oh, brother! Their famous last two words almost slay me. After Christ asked, "Can you drink the cup I drink or be baptized with the baptism I am baptized with?" they answered without hesitation: "We can." They didn't have any idea what they were talking about because they didn't have any idea what Christ was talking about. Soon they would. And one day in the distant future they would sip from the cup and know the baptism of His suffering; but in their present state, they needed a baby bottle. Not a cup.

Our problem is often the same as theirs. We let the human image of Christ mislead us into downsizing Him. "If He'd just stoop a little and we stood on our tiptoes, we'd be just about side by side. One at His left. One at His right." Negatory, Good Buddy. When the Word became flesh to dwell among us, human flesh wrapped its way around "the fullness of the Godhead bodily" (Col. 2:9, KJV).

Because of the Lord's great love we are not consumed.
—Lamentations 3:22

How did Isaiah react to His election, call, and revelation in Isaiah 6:5?

"Woe to me!" I cried. "I am ruined! For I am a man of unclean lips, and I live among a people of unclean lips, and my eyes have seen the King, the Lord Almighty."
—Isaiah 6:5

John 12:41 tells us that Isaiah saw Jesus' glory. I am convinced if we, present company included, really "got" the concept of being chosen and called by Jesus Christ the divine Son of God, we'd be too humbled to get up and "go"! Like the Prophet Ezekiel, the Spirit of God would have to set us on our feet for us to get off our faces. (See Ezek. 2:1-2.) Yes, we've been chosen; and, yes, we've been called. But we'll know we're grasping the concept when our humanity is cloaked in humility.

He said to me, "Son of man, stand up on your feet and I will speak to you." As he spoke, the Spirit came into me and raised me to my feet, and I heard him speaking to me.
—Ezekiel 2:1-2

1. Matthew Henry, *Matthew to John, vol. 5* in *Matthew Henry's Commentary on the Whole Bible* (New York: Fleming H. Revell Company), 456.

REFLECTION

HOW DO YOU SHOW HUMILITY IN YOUR RELATIONSHIPS?

Chapter Two
THE REALITY OF THE COMMITMENT

A disciple commits to taking up his or her cross and following Jesus.

KEY SCRIPTURE

ONE OF THEM, THE DISCIPLE WHOM JESUS LOVED, WAS RECLINING NEXT TO HIM. —JOHN 13:23

Reclining Next to Jesus

The final week of Christ's life as the God-man started exactly as the disciples preferred: with the fanfare of a triumphal entry. The week of the great feast had arrived, and so many Jews were in Jerusalem that a donkey couldn't even hear himself neigh. Surely the disciples had joined their families in many pilgrimages to the holy city to observe the Passover, but this year they attended with One who appeared to be the Master of Ceremonies. Their impatient, ambitious feet seemed finally about to enter the big time on pay dirt. They were about to be important. Or at least, that's what they thought.

JESUS WEPT OVER A CITY THAT DESPERATELY NEEDED GOD. HAS YOUR HEART EVER BEEN BROKEN BECAUSE SOMEONE WILL NOT ACKNOWLEDGE JESUS? EXPLAIN.

Jesus' Reaction to the City

Word had traveled quickly that Jesus was on His way to the city, so a crowd had gathered to meet Him, waving palm branches and shouting, "Hosanna! Blessed is he who comes in the name of the Lord! Blessed is the King of Israel!" (John 12:13)

Then, right in the middle of the parade approaching Jerusalem, Jesus took a good look at the city and cried. Luke 19:41 simply tells us that Jesus wept over it, but the Greek word used for *wept* is the strongest word for *grief* in the original New Testament text. The wording suggests that His grief was not only deep but also demonstrative. Take a look at Luke 19:41-44 and then leave your Bible open at this passage.

Imagine Peter, James, and John standing close by and glancing at one another. Perhaps they even shrugged their shoulders. Just about the time they thought He had pulled Himself together, however, He startled them again. Read what Jesus did next according to Luke 19:45-46.

Preparation for the Feast

Luke 19:47–21:38 gives us a glimpse of Christ teaching in the temple on Monday, Tuesday, and Wednesday. Then the day of Unleavened Bread came, the day on which Jews sacrificed the Passover lamb. Read Luke 22:7-13 and notice the task He assigned to Peter and John.

Christ's appointments are never haphazard. He can accomplish anything He desires by merely thinking it into existence. That He assigns us to certain tasks implies that our experience is often as important as the task. Sometimes more so. I believe not only that Peter and John were chosen for the job of preparing the Passover but also that the job was chosen for them. In their letters to the churches, Peter and John frequently refer to Christ as "the Lamb."

Jesus would not rest until He taught Peter and John exactly what that title meant. The pair didn't run by the old city market and grab a wrapped package of trimmed lamb for a buck-fifty a pound. They picked out a live lamb and had the sweet thing slaughtered. Very likely they held it still for the knife. You and I can hardly imagine all that was involved in preparing for a Passover, but you can be sure that none of it was wasted on Peter and John. That's one of the things I love about Christ. If He gives us a difficult task, every ounce of our experience is meant for our instruction and growth, if only we'll let Him finish the work.

The Meaning of the Passover

I believe as Peter and John prepared the Passover meal that day, they were privy to many secrets that became clearer to them as time passed. Ecclesiastes 3:11 says that God makes everything beautiful in its time. I truly believe that if we're willing to see, God uses every difficulty and every assignment to confide deep things to us, and that the lessons are not complete until their beauty is revealed. I fear, however, that we are so often attention deficit that we settle for bearable when beauty is just around the corner.

Surely the Holy Spirit helped Peter and John fully understand the profound significance of the Passover in which Jesus became the Lamb. John never could get over it. From the pen of an elderly, shaking hand we find more than 20 references to the Lamb in the Book of Revelation. And it was Peter, his sidekick, who wrote, "You know that it was not with perishable things such as silver or gold that you were redeemed from the empty way of life handed down to you from your forefathers, but with the precious blood of Christ, a lamb without blemish or defect" (1 Pet. 1:18-19).

When I think of a Jewish heritage, I imagine anything but empty! We Americans lack the rich traditions of other cultures. Who could have enjoyed richer ways of life and more tradition than what was handed down by Jewish forefathers to their sons and daughters? Yet Peter called them empty. Why? I think because once Peter saw their fulfillment in Jesus Christ, he knew the traditions were empty without Jesus. Once he knew the true Passover Lamb, an Old Testament Passover meant nothing without its fulfillment in Jesus. Jesus became everything, and all former things were empty without Him. Thank goodness for the patience of Christ to make all things beautiful over time.

Leaning on Jesus

Let's conclude with a snapshot moment. Jesus told His disciples that one among them would betray Him.

Read John 13:23-25. We will save our comments on the expression "the disciple whom Jesus loved"; but assuming he is our John, what was his place at the table?

> One of them, the disciple whom Jesus loved, was reclining next to him. Simon Peter motioned to this disciple and said, "Ask him which one he means." Leaning back against Jesus, he asked him, "Lord, who is it?"
>
> —John 13:23-25

You have just stumbled onto the chief clue that scholars use to identify John as the youngest disciple. At the traditional Jewish Passover, the youngest child at the table who is able to talk often sits nearest the father or father figure and asks the traditional questions.

I love imagining that the younger among them might have acted like he felt, not just how he felt was proper. Hence his leaning against Jesus. Glory! You see, there's just nothing doctrinal about John's leaning on Jesus. It wasn't the law. It wasn't in the proverbial Passover Book of Rules. John didn't have to lean on Jesus to talk to Him. Christ could hear him just fine. John leaned on Him because he wanted to. Because he loved Him. Because Jesus was … leanable. Approachable. Downright lovable. Be still my heart. I cannot wait.

One of our primary tasks through this journey is to explore the deep affection that flowed like a teeming brook between Jesus and John. I'll be honest with you. I want what they had. If a mortal can experience it with the Immortal Invisible, I want it. I want "to know this love that surpasses knowledge—that [I] may be filled to the measure of all the fullness of God" (Eph. 3:19). All else is just an empty way of life handed down by bored and unmotivated forefathers. No thanks. Give me Jesus.

🌴 Sleeping in a Garden 🌴

Few things shake us to the core like the sudden revelation of a Judas. Maybe because we can't believe we didn't see it coming. Maybe because we're terrified that if one of the disciples could be a Judas, couldn't we all? Aren't we all self-centered, vain, and ambitious? Didn't he say, "Surely not I" like the rest? We are terrified by our similarities! And rightly we should be.

The Betrayal

But one thing sets us apart from Judas.
Read John 13:21-30. What happened as soon as Judas took the bread?

That's right. Satan entered into Judas. John 13:28 tells us that no one at the meal understood. Over the course of years and countless replays of the scene in the mind of the apostle John, he knew the devil entered into Judas at that table right before his very eyes. How did he know? Christ taught in John 14:26 that the Holy Spirit is also the holy Reminder. He can reveal the truth through an event that happened in the past, clarifying what He was teaching us that we were unable to grasp at the time. Jesus often teaches us lessons that He knows we won't fully understand until later.

Try to grasp that Judas was not inhabited by any old demon from hell. Satan is not omnipresent; he can only be in one place at a time. For that time, he was in Judas. Satan flew like a fiery dart into the willing vessel of one of the twelve.

Oh, we can follow. Closely. And still not belong to Jesus. We can talk the talk. We can blend right in. We can seem so sincere.

I believe through the videotape of his own memory, John saw the devil in Judas' eyes. I think he saw him in Judas' hand as he reached for the dipped bread. Think about it. For the briefest moment, two hands held the same bread. One was soiled by silver. The other was a thin glove of flesh cloaking the hand of God. John saw the devil in Judas' feet as he walked away. When we are truly Christ's, we can never leave Him.

The Betrayer's Fate

Later the same hands that betrayed Christ would tie a knot in a rope and loop it around his own neck (Matt. 27:5). Those same feet would spasm and jerk, then dangle lifelessly. I think perhaps Judas took his own life because the devil he betrayed Christ to please then betrayed him. The devil used him and left him. Judas did not even have the dignity of a warrior of hell. He was discarded like a soiled rag. Less than nothing. That's Satan's way. He is friend to no one. He only pretends. He is the Betrayer.

The important thing to remember is that we must not let Satan beat us up to the point of harming ourselves when we fall for one of his traps. As long as we're alive, there is always hope and the possibility of restoration through God's grace. I am a walking testimony of this fact. We have only to seek this restoration.

KEY SCRIPTURE

HE TOOK PETER AND THE TWO SONS OF ZEBEDEE ALONG WITH HIM, AND HE BEGAN TO BE SORROWFUL AND TROUBLED.
—MATTHEW 26:37

REFLECTION

HAS THE DEVIL EVER BETRAYED YOU? HAS HE EVER TALKED YOU INTO SOMETHING AND USED YOU, THEN LEFT YOU DANGLING?

The Mount of Olives

Soon after Judas departed that night, Christ and His disciples observed the ordinance of the New Covenant, sang a hymn, and went to the Mount of Olives. (See Matt. 26:30.) Again, what they could not grasp in Jesus' teaching of the bread and the wine, the holy Reminder would later explain to them.

The Mount of Olives was perched east and directly across from Jerusalem overlooking the temple. In ancient times the whole mount must have been covered with dense olive groves. According to Luke 22:39, Jesus had been to the Mount of Olives often. Unlike the disciples who took the steep walk beside Him, as Jesus climbed that hill He knew its significance—both past and future. The previous Sunday, He had baptized the Mount of Olives with His tears as he cried, "If you, even you, had only known on this day what would bring you peace!" (Luke 19:42) On this most profound of all Passover nights, He would baptize the Mount of Olives with sweat like drops of blood falling to the ground. Read Matthew 26:36-46. Did you notice that Peter, James, and John were once again drawn out from the others?

Gethsemane is the third time Peter, James, and John were eyewitnesses to a scene the others did not observe. I think we can rest assured the disciples had never seen Jesus like the three saw Him in Gethsemane. I have studied this scene many times before but never from the point of view of the disciples.

Jesus represented security and strength to His disciples. Grown men don't follow someone for three years with virtually no income unless they are completely taken with Him. I believe Jesus was their whole lives. In Him their pasts made sense. Their present lives were totally immersed in Him, and all their hopes for the future rested in His faithfulness to do what He promised. And indeed He would … but never in a million years would they have expected how. Jesus told them, "My soul is overwhelmed with sorrow to the point of death. Stay here and keep watch with me" (Matt. 26:38).

Wait a second! This was their Rock! Their Strong Tower! Can't you just hear their questions: "What in the world is wrong with Him? Why is He on the ground like that? Why is His hair drenched in sweat?"

When was the last time you saw someone you consider to be a "rock" in unabashed anguish, virtually inconsolable, and overwhelmed with sorrow? Describe how you felt.

God … on His Knees

The disciples may not have realized that Jesus was no less God that moment than He was on the Mount of Transfiguration. He was no less God than He was when He raised the dead. Their Rock and their Strong Tower was not falling apart. He was falling on His knees. That takes strength. There in the Garden, the Son of God bore His private cross. Very soon He would bear it publicly; but when He rose from knees bruised with anguish, His face, dusted with earth, was set like flint. I want to leave you with one last point that I find critical to our understanding about the heart of God. Christ knew what He was going to have to do when He came to earth.

Remember? He was as good as dead from the beginning. Jesus lived for one purpose alone: to do the will of His Father. Yet He still felt.

Jesus is the precise image of His Father, who also feels. God is holy. God is righteous. Our salvation necessitates a cross. Our poor decisions necessitate chastisement. The refusal of the lost to believe necessitates judgment. But God still feels. Beloved, God still feels.

And so will we. Sometimes obeying God in a matter will be the hardest thing we've ever done in our lives. We are not wrong to feel. We are wrong to disobey. Hash it out with God. Ask for the cup to be removed. But resolve to do His will, no matter what. Glory is at stake. That's why Jesus drew the three close enough to see. To teach them to pray … not sleep … in their anguish. This time they slept. They had little power to do otherwise. But a time would come when each would rise from his own Gethsemane and bear his own cross.

KEY SCRIPTURE

WHEN JESUS SAW HIS MOTHER THERE, AND THE DISCIPLE WHOM HE LOVED STANDING NEARBY, HE SAID TO HIS MOTHER, "DEAR WOMAN, HERE IS YOUR SON," AND TO THE DISCIPLE, "HERE IS YOUR MOTHER." —JOHN 19:26-27

Standing Near the Cross

Have you ever looked around you at circumstances and thought, *How did I get here?* I remember feeling that way when I sat with Keith's family in the ICU waiting room while his beautiful 23-year-old sister lay dying with an aneurysm. Just a few nights earlier we had been laughing until our sides split. Suddenly in a string of events that happened with staggering speed, our entire lives changed. No Broadway stage could have captured the raw, gaping emotions of this real-life drama. Those were days I desperately wished to delete from the calendar and just go back to life like it was.

When was the last time you felt this way?

Going through such anguish gives us some idea of the way John must have felt in the scene depicted by John 19:17-27. Read these Scriptures. Don't you know he wished someone would wake him up from his nightmare? This scene captures a profoundly tender and emotional exchange between Jesus, John, and Mary; but don't tag it a warm and fuzzy moment and try to snuggle up to it. The events John observed were horrific. We can appreciate the depth of the tenderness only against the backdrop of the horror. You may have studied the cross of Christ in the past, but today we are going to attempt to capture it from the exact angle where the apostle John's sandals flattened the dirt.

The Arrest

Let's rewind the events to place John accurately in the scenes. We know without a doubt John was an eyewitness to the events described in John 18:1-11. Read these verses. Put yourself in John's place. Imagine what you would have been thinking as you watched an entire detachment of soldiers carrying torches, lanterns, and weapons up the hill.

To me, one of the most amazing moments in the final hours of Christ's life happened when He answered their demand for Jesus of Nazareth by saying, "I am he" and the crowd drew back and fell to the ground. The word *he* doesn't appear in the original Greek. I believe they experienced a compulsory buckling of the knees because the Son of God announced the name by which God said He'd be remembered throughout all generations: "I Am!" (Ex. 3:14-15) John himself recorded this scene.

We are told an important detail in John 18:15. Many scholars believe the words "another disciple" refer to John. Notice what he alone did. Several of the disciples followed from a distance, but John appeared to have been the closest eyewitness of the twelve as the final hours unfolded. Read John 19:1-16.

The Trial

Did you notice the word *finally* in verse 16? Pilate finally handed Christ over after they had tossed Him back and forth from court to court like a ball in a tennis match. Finally a public road was about to be paved into the holy of holies (the most sacred place in the temple, associated with God's presence, only the high priest could enter and only once a year). Finally a perfect, unblemished Lamb would be sacrificed to fulfill the righteous requirements of the temple's blazing altar. Finally something would happen to reconcile believing man to God once and for all. After thousands of years of man's folly, someone in a cloak of flesh did it right. Finally! Glory to God!

We don't know how distant John was forced to remain, but can you imagine the verdict filtering through the ranks? "Jesus is going to be crucified." "The verdict is in: crucifixion!" They all knew too well what crucifixion entailed. It was the worst nightmare of anyone alive in that part of the world. At a time when any thinking man would want to run for his life, John, probably the youngest of all the disciples, stayed.

Near the Cross

That's what the Gospel of John says. Read John 19:25-27 again. Above the young man hung his world. His Leader. His Hero. His Future. Three years earlier he was minding his own business trying to gain his daddy's approval with a boat and a net. He hadn't asked for Jesus. Jesus asked for him. And here he stood. Isaiah's startling prophecy tells us that by the time the foes of Jesus finished with Him, His appearance was disfigured beyond human likeness. Read Isaiah 52:14.

From the cross, Jesus saw His mother standing there with John. "Dear woman, here is your son," He told His mother. Don't take it lightly. Hear it. Hear a voice erupting from labored outburst as Jesus tried to lift Himself up and draw breath to speak. Every word He said from the cross is critical by virtue of the fact that Jesus' condition made speech harder than dying. Chronic pain is jealous like few other things. It doesn't like to share. If a man is in pain, he can hardly think of anything else; yet Jesus did. I think perhaps He did because the pain of His heart, if at all possible, exceeded the pain of His shredded frame. He saw the look on His mother's face. Her horror. Her suffering.

Then Jesus gazed straight upon the young face of the one standing nearby. "Here is your mother," He said to John.

> God said to Moses, "I Am Who I Am.... This is my name forever, the name by which I am to be remembered from generation to generation."—Exodus 3:14-15

> There were many who were appalled at him—his appearance was so disfigured beyond that of any man and his form marred beyond human likeness.
> –Isaiah 52:14

How perfectly appropriate! We're about to discover the very element that set the apostle John apart from all the rest right at the foot of the cross. I am a huge fan of the apostle Peter and can relate with him far more readily than John, but the inspired words the Holy Spirit later entrusted to the Son of Thunder suggest a profound uniqueness.

I am convinced we've stumbled on the very thing that set John apart and made him the fertile soil into which God could sow the seeds of the gospel. John remained nearby Jesus whether his Leader was on the Mount of Transfiguration or in the depths of Gethsemane's suffering. John leaned affectionately upon Him during the feast but also followed Him into the courts for the trials. John clung to Jesus when He raised the dead, and he clung to Jesus when He became the dead. The young disciple stayed nearby during Christ's brightest hour and His darkest hour.

We cannot claim to know anyone intimately whom we've not known in the intensity of both agony and elation. Anyone with eyes willing to truly behold Jesus will at times be confused and shocked by what he sees. You see, if we're willing to be taken to the extremities of His glory where intimate knowledge is gained, we will undoubtedly see things of Him we cannot explain and that sometimes disturb. Then comes the question: Will we walk away from Jesus when from human understanding He looks weak and defeated? Do you know what I mean by that question? What do we do when we can't explain what Jesus is doing? Will we remain nearby when He hasn't stopped a tragedy? When based on earthly evidence, human reasoning is left to one of two harrowing conclusions: He is either mean or weak. Will we stand by faith when human logic says to run?

That is what will make us different.

REFLECTION

HOW CLOSE ARE YOU STAYING TO JESUS? WILL YOU KEEP CLINGING TO HIM IN THE WORST TIMES WHEN YOU CANNOT UNDERSTAND?

KEY SCRIPTURE

PETER AND THE OTHER DISCIPLE STARTED FOR THE TOMB. BOTH WERE RUNNING, BUT THE OTHER DISCIPLE OUTRAN PETER AND REACHED THE TOMB FIRST. —JOHN 20:3-4

"I tell you the truth, unless a kernel of wheat falls to the ground and dies, it remains only a single seed. But if it dies, it produces many seeds."—John 12:24

Racing to the Tomb

When all was completed, Jesus said, "It is finished." He then bowed His head and gave up His spirit. (See John 19:28,30.) Watching someone we love suffer violent pain causes us to feel unbridled relief when it ends, even if death is what bids it to cease. Then true to our self-destructive natures, relief often gives way to guilt. To add to the heap, the finality of the death ushers in feelings of hopelessness.

Kernel of Wheat

Read the words of Christ echoing from the grave in John 12:24. As a child bearing the name of Christ, if a part of you has died, in time it was meant to produce many seeds.

We hear so much talk about the phases of grief: the shock; the anger; often depression; then finally, acceptance … if we're lucky. We're led to believe that acceptance of the death is the final stage of grief; but if we're in Christ, the final stage has not come until we've allowed God to bring forth resurrection life and many seeds from the kernel of wheat that fell to the ground.

The Empty Tomb

Read John's own account of the events that occurred early on the first day of the week in John 20:1-18. Again, we are pretty safe to assume that "the other disciple" in this scene is John himself.

We have no idea where Mary found Peter and John, but she found them together, as usual. They were dear friends, weren't they? They most likely had known each other all their lives. For the last three years they had lived the great adventure together. They had seen things people would not even believe. And now they had seen something they themselves couldn't believe. They saw their fearless Leader beaten to a bloody pulp and nailed to a criminal's cross. Jesus was dead. And to top it off, missing.

"They have taken the Lord out of the tomb, and we don't know…" Their feet began moving before their minds could think. They were running. Harder. Faster. Hearts pounding. Adrenaline pumping. Fear surging. "Where is He?"

They had walked side by side for years. Now they ran side by side. At this emotionally heightened moment in Scripture, I am amused at the man in John to incidentally tell us that he outran Peter. Ever competitive, aren't men? Then the same youth that outran Peter appeared to have chickened out on going into the tomb. Can you just imagine Peter saying, "Come on, John! It's OK. Mary was right. No one's here. But look at this!" Strips of linen were lying there.

The Resurrection

The Father had waited long enough on that first Easter morning. He didn't even let the sun come up. Suddenly the Lord God Omnipotent raised His mighty arm and unleashed strength beyond comprehension. Somehow I don't think the cold, lifeless body of Christ gradually grew warm. No, I'm convinced the blood flashed red-hot through His veins and He stood to His feet so fast the grave clothes couldn't stick to Him. Clothed in resurrection raiment, Christ Jesus the Savior of the world stepped out of the tomb. Matthew 28:2-4 gives us insight into what happened next.

I've been called the "Drama Queen" more than a few times. May I have the honor of presenting to you God Almighty, the King of Drama? Compared to Him, I'm nothing but a knot on a log. He's got the drama thing going, and I for one don't want to be caught sitting when a standing ovation is in order.

Seeing Jesus Again

Let's look again at John 20. Recall that Mary tarried long enough to see the resurrected Lord Jesus face-to-face. Read verses 17 and 18 again. How I thank God that He appointed His Son to bring such dignity to women. Especially one like me who had been so defeated and disturbed in her past. In a very tender way, Mary was the very first one Christ sent forth to bring the best news of all: Jesus is alive!

Now read John 20:19-23. Picture the scene. We are told in the previous verse that Mary took the news just as Christ instructed. We have no reason to believe John had yet laid eyes on Him. Sit back and imagine the room. Feel the oppression of fear in the air. Picture the bars across

REFLECTION

WHAT DOES THE RESURRECTION MEAN TO YOU?

There was a violent earthquake, for an angel of the Lord came down from heaven and, going to the tomb, rolled back the stone and sat on it. His appearance was like lightning, and his clothes were white as snow. The guards were so afraid of him that they shook and became like dead men.
–Matthew 28:2-4

the doors and the captives inside who only a short time before wielded power to cast out demons and heal the sick. Had they been stripped of their authority or their abilities? No indeed. Powerlessness is an effect of the message of fear the enemy (Satan) brings.

Suddenly Jesus walked right through their barriers and appeared among them. I've been there. I bet you have, too. Like a father has compassion on his children, so Jesus has compassion on us. (See Ps. 103:13.) He knew what their finite minds needed, so He showed them His hands and side. Have you ever noticed how we constantly expect people to heal from the beatings of life and lose their scars? I'm somehow comforted to know that Christ still has His.

Picture the expressions on their faces. Feel the oppression lift in the glorious imposition of electric life. Now look around the scene of your imagination and find our friend, the apostle John. Wait for a moment, even a few seconds, when Jesus' eyes may have fastened on him alone. Somehow in my imagination, I see young John's eyebrows pinned to his hairline, eyes peeled as big as saucers. I think he probably froze for a second until the love of Christ melted him like butter. Then I wonder if he broke out in such a toothy grin that Jesus wanted to laugh. Someone as young as John probably was not only thinking the same things as the others, he might have been thinking … perhaps even saying, "We won!" And indeed they had. They had won Christ.

KEY SCRIPTURE

WHEN PETER SAW [JOHN], HE ASKED, "LORD, WHAT ABOUT HIM?"—JOHN 21:21

⫷ Following at a Distance ⫸

One of the post-resurrection images of Christ I love most is when He told Mary Magdalene to peel herself from Him in John 20:17 so that each of them could be released to do what God called them to do. The moment Mary recognized Jesus, she obviously latched onto Him for dear life as if to say, "Now that I've found you, I will never let you go!"

I don't doubt that once the disciples saw their resurrected Savior, they wanted to hang onto Him just as tightly as Mary Magdalene. And they were just as unable. According to Acts 1:3, Christ stayed on planet earth to reveal Himself for only 40 days after He rose from the dead.

Return to Fishing

Today we're going to sit on the shore of the Sea of Galilee, also called the Sea of Tiberias, and watch one of the last encounters between Christ and the disciples. Although the spotlight seems to be on Peter, I want you to focus on John's role in the events described. Read John 21:1-14.

Peter and the others obviously had returned to fishing. It seems Peter ascribed to the philosophy: when you don't know what to do, do what you used to do. The fact that Jesus didn't hang around must have been confusing to them. I'm not sure they knew how they fit into Christ's work from this side of the grave. Surely the thought occurred to them, "What need does anyone powerful enough to walk out of a tomb have for the likes of us?" They didn't understand that Christ's primary purpose during those 40 days was for people to understand He was God.

Keep in mind, Jesus had more on His agenda than appearing only to His disciples. According to 1 Corinthians 15:5-7, He revealed Himself to more than 500 of His followers.

What does Psalm 46:10 tell us we're supposed to do when God is revealing Himself to people?

"Be still, and know that I am God; I will be exalted among the nations, I will be exalted in the earth."—Psalm 46:10

Be still. Don't default into the past. Don't jump the gun for the future. Just behold and know. Instructions will come when the time is right. In the meantime, being is so much harder than doing, isn't it?

John seemed to have a better grasp on what Christ had come to be than any of the others at this point. He is attributed only four words in this scene in John 21. What are they?

_____ _____ _____ _____!

Jumping Overboard

The second John announced Jesus, Peter jumped from the boat and swam to Him with all his might. I realize our primary attentions are on John in this study, but I can't let this moment pass without putting the flashlight on one of Peter's sterling moments.

In our Christian circles we so often surround ourselves with people of similar practice of faith. We have our unspoken codes, our spiritual practices that we consider acceptable. We also agree on things that are not. Things that are weird. Behaviors that are just … well … overboard. Then someone among us jumps ship and decides he doesn't care what the rest of us think. Nothing is going to get between him and Jesus. Glory! As much as I love John, in this scene I want to be Peter!

Actually, I remember well when I began to break the unspoken code of just how far my church compadres and I would go with this "spiritual thing." Years ago those closest to me charged me with going overboard. Do you know what, Beloved? I wouldn't climb back in that boat for anything.

How about you? Have you jumped out of the boat of what is most comfortable and acceptable and decided you want Jesus even if you have to make a fool of yourself to get to Him? If so, elaborate. If not, are you ready? What's holding you back?

REFLECTION

IS YOUR FAITH AN "OVERBOARD" KIND OF FAITH OR ARE YOU PRETTY MUCH STILL IN THE BOAT?

I believe Jesus esteemed Peter's passionate determination to get to his Lord. I am also convinced that this act was an important part of Peter's restoration. Notice he didn't ask to walk on water. He was willing to dog paddle in ice water to get to Jesus this time. His leap from the boat may have suggested that at this point Peter truly loved Christ more than these.

Now read John 21:15-23, looking for John in the snapshot. I love this scene because it represents something of a do-over to me. What did Christ say to Peter in verse 19?

Three years earlier Peter heard the same words and, to his credit, he had done it. But he had done it in his own strength and with his own agenda. His own ambition.

Remember what happened the last time in Scripture Peter warmed himself by a fire? (See Luke 22:55-57.) What was the obvious motivation Christ wanted for Peter's "follow-ship" in the John 21 discourse?

    _____ Lordship   _____ Love   _____ Leadership

Oh, Beloved, can you see the significance? No other motivation will last! We might feed the sheep or serve the flock based on other motivations for a while, but only one thing will compel us to follow the Lord Jesus Christ faithfully to the death: love!

You see, our callings may differ; but if we're going to follow Jesus Christ in the power of the crucified life, our motivation will be the same. Only love compels to the death. Dear one, life is hard. Opposition is huge. Circumstances will inevitably happen in all our lives that will defy all discipline, determination, and conviction. Love keeps burning when everything else disintegrates in an ashen heap. Pray for this one thing more than you pray for your next breath. Love is everything.

And John Followed

A young disciple named John was so drawn to Christ's discourse on love that he couldn't help but listen as Jesus and Peter walked away from the others to talk. I am convinced the conversation recorded in John 21:15-23 began in the group of eight. Perhaps in the course of the question and answer, Jesus quite naturally stood up, brushed Himself off, and took a few steps away from the small circle of men. Peter, unnerved by his own interpretation of the repetitive question, probably jumped to his feet and followed.

The King James Version tells us that Peter was grieved because Jesus questioned his love a third time. "Lord, You know all things; You know that I love You." Mind you, he was still drenched to the bone from his zeal. Jesus then prophesied the reason why Peter's love for Him would be so critical. Peter would be asked to glorify God by giving his own life in a painful death. Only love would make him willing.

Then, as if to say, "Knowing all this and with your eyes wide open," Christ re-issued the call, "Follow Me!" Don't downplay it for an instant. The cost of the call was huge. We don't know what caused Peter to suddenly look behind him and see John following them. Perhaps John stepped on a branch that had fallen to the ground. Perhaps he groaned audibly when he heard Christ foretell his closest friend's future.

I don't believe John trailed them out of selfish curiosity. I think he sensed the enormity of the concept the risen Teacher was teaching through this emotional interchange. This was no tiptoed eavesdropping. I think he was drawn to the conversation like a magnet. I believe Scripture will prove that John, perhaps like no other disciple in that circle, understood what his beloved Savior was saying. "You are My called ones. You have tough futures ahead of you; but the glory God will gain will be immeasurable. Love is the only motivation that can afford this kind of cost." Notice what Peter asked Jesus when he saw John (v. 21).

At times like these I wish we had the Bible on videotape! We would be far better equipped to interpret a scene accurately if we could see the expressions on the face of the speaker and hear his tone of voice. Since we have no such help, words like Peter's may have as many different interpretations as I have commentaries.

Do you think Peter's question was out of deep concern for John, or did it arise out of jealousy or some other emotion?

REFLECTION

WHEN IS THE LAST TIME YOU TRUSTED GOD IN A DIFFICULT SITUATION? YOU CAN BE SURE THAT DIFFICULT DAYS LIE AHEAD. HOW WILL YOU FACE THEM?

No matter what your interpretation may be, I think we can all admit that this question plagues us as well. Perhaps you have served side by side with someone and God has called you to suffer some pretty difficult circumstances while that person has seemed to flourish in relative ease. Or perhaps your heart has broken for someone who works so hard and has served so diligently but difficulty is her constant companion.

Now read Christ's response in John 21:22. Beloved, over and over Jesus tells us, "You can trust Me!" In this scene He is saying to His present-day disciples, "You can trust Me with you, and you can trust Me with them. I am the same God to all of you, but I have a different plan for each of you. You won't miss it if you keep following. Remember, I've been a carpenter by trade. Custom blueprints are My specialty. God's glory is My goal. You're not ready until you'd swim it … or walk it … all by yourself. Now, fill your canteen to the brim with love and follow Me."

Chapter Three
THE CALL TO A PERSONAL MINISTRY

Jesus calls us to use our gifts to serve Him in a unique ministry.

KEY SCRIPTURE

YOU WILL RECEIVE
POWER WHEN THE
HOLY SPIRIT COMES
ON YOU; AND
YOU WILL BE MY
WITNESSES.
—ACTS 1:8

⤖⬥ On a Mountain Top ⤖⬥

Today you and I are going to stand on the sidelines and watch the disciples experience some pretty wild things, yet they happened just as Scripture says they did. You see, the testimony of the Word of Truth makes what seems incredible perfectly credible. Our reading will take place in three parts today.

You Will Receive Power

Begin by reading Acts 1:1-12. I am convinced we can as readily apply verse 8 to ourselves as we can to Christ's original disciples. Fill in the blanks below with your name.

"But _____ will receive power when the Holy Spirit comes on _____."

The Holy Spirit comes no other way but in power. Read 2 Corinthians 4:7. The "treasure" Paul was touting is the Holy Spirit. Notice God's goal in giving us this Treasure.

Beloved, God wants to hang out all over you! Don't you see? That's why our circumstances and challenges are often beyond us! If life were completely manageable, we'd manage on our own strength, and no one would see the living proof of God's existence in us. We were left here for the distinct purpose of becoming witnesses to an injured world in desperate need of a Savior. Do you belong to Jesus Christ? If so, the Holy Spirit dwells in you (Rom. 8:9); and He did not cheat you of a single ounce of His power.

After Christ assured the disciples of the coming power of the Holy Spirit, He was taken up to heaven and a cloud hid Him from their sight. Imagine the scene from the apostle John's viewpoint. There he was, eye-to-eye with Jesus, not letting a single word from His mouth fall on deaf ears. Then he realized that he was glancing somewhat upward as Jesus seemed a tad taller. As Jesus rose a head above the group, surely John looked down and saw that His feet were no longer on the ground. Had my grandmother been one of the disciples (a frighteningly funny thought), she would have stood there saying, "Now, don't that just beat all?" I feel sure they said something comparable in Hebrew.

Back in the Upstairs Room

Let's look briefly at our second reading segment in Acts 1:12-26. Remember, most of the disciples were from the villages around the Sea of Galilee. Scripture tells us their return to the city was a "Sabbath day's walk," which would have been about three-fourths of a mile. I have walked that brief trek. It is straight downhill. You can hardly keep from walking fast due to the incline, but somehow I'm imagining their mouths were traveling faster than their feet. The disciples went upstairs to the room where they were staying. A few days later, others joined the disciples in this room.

How large was that first New Testament cell group according to Acts 1:15?
___25 ___50 ___120 ___500

You may attend a church about this size and wonder with frustration what God could do with such a small group of people. Dear One, when the Holy Spirit falls on a place, it doesn't matter how small the group; things start happening! Remember, the Holy Spirit comes in order to get results!

The Day of Pentecost

Let's find out what can happen when the Holy Spirit interrupts a prayer meeting. Your final reading today is Acts 2:1-21. Read it carefully.

We have this treasure in jars of clay to show that this all-surpassing power is from God and not from us.—2 Corinthians 4:7

REFLECTION

WHAT IMPACT DID THE HOLY SPIRIT HAVE THE LAST TIME YOU FELT HIM MOVE IN YOUR HEART?

You need to review some Jewish history so you can understand the significance of this event. God appointed annual feasts to be observed in honor of Him. The most important of the Jewish feasts was (and is) Passover, which recalls the time of Israelite captivity in Egypt. The Lord "passed over" the homes of Israelites, sparing their lives. The first born of each Egyptian home died. (See Ex. 12.) The feast that immediately followed was Firstfruits, when a sheaf of the first grain of the harvest was waved before the Lord for His acceptance (Lev. 23:16). This was the day after the Passover Sabbath, obviously falling on a Sunday. Fifty days after Passover came the Feast of Weeks, later called Pentecost. Pentecost was a celebration of the harvest reaped for seven weeks.

Do you see the significance of what happened on this Pentecost described in Acts 2? Fifty days earlier, Christ, the Passover Lamb, was crucified. On the day of Firstfruits, the next Sunday morning, His life was waved before God for His acceptance as the Firstfruit from the dead. Then on Pentecost, the Holy Spirit came just as Christ promised His disciples.

The Holy Spirit reveals Himself in countless ways in Scripture. How did He reveal His all-surpassing power that day?

Those who accepted his message were baptized, and about three thousand were added to their number that day.—Acts 2:41

The Holy Spirit never comes just to show off. He comes to bring results.

What were the results on that first Pentecost after Christ our Passover Lamb was offered, according to Acts 2:41?

Beloved, I present to you the first harvest reaped by the life, death, and resurrection of Jesus Christ our Lord. That's Pentecost! And even now I believe we are still living in a type of Pentecost. Christ waits only so that the harvest can reach its peak ripeness and be reaped to the glory of God. He does not will for any to perish but wants all to come to repentance. (See 2 Pet. 3:9.) He desires everyone. He forces no one. He will not wait forever. One day the ultimate Feast of Trumpets (Lev. 23:23-24; 1 Thess. 4:16) will come, and we will meet Jesus in the air. One day the Book will be opened and closed for the last time, and the final judgment will take place. (See Rev. 20:11-15.) Those covered by the blood of the Lamb (Jesus) will dwell with God forever and ever ... and so shall we ever be with the Lord. (See 1 Cor. 5:7 and 1 Thess. 4:17.) Glory! I feel like celebrating a little early.

🌴 At the Temple 🌴

Read all of Acts 3, focusing on the first 13 verses. What you have before you in this chapter of Scripture is a pair of mighty fine servants. Allow me to highlight five things I love about Peter and John in this scene.

KEY SCRIPTURE

PETER SAID, "SILVER OR GOLD I DO NOT HAVE, BUT WHAT I HAVE I GIVE YOU. IN THE NAME OF JESUS CHRIST OF NAZARETH, WALK."—ACTS 3:6

Jesus Fulfilled Jewish Heritage

First of all, they cherished their heritage. Please don't miss the fact that the New Testament church was Jewish! Acts 3 opens with Peter and John on their way to the three o'clock prayer time at the temple. The thought never occurred to them to cast off their Judaism for their new faith in Christ. For heaven's sake, Jesus was Jewish! Nothing could have been more absurd. Their Messiah fulfilled their Jewish heritage. They were no longer obligated to the letter of the law because Christ had met its righteous requirements.

Can you imagine how belief in Christ and their newfound knowledge of Jesus as the answer to every symbolic Jewish practice spiced up their participation? Suddenly the black and white of their ritual prayer services turned Technicolor with the life of the Spirit.

They Looked Suffering in the Face

Second, Peter and John were not so busy getting to prayer meeting that they missed the beggar at the gate. Don't miss the significance of the location being the gate called Beautiful. Leave it to God to appoint a bitter reality in our "beautiful" scene. Try as we may to avoid misery, misfortune, and injustice around us, they will find us. My city is filled with gated and extravagant "planned communities" with walls around them to keep the niceties in and the unpleasantries out. I don't have a single problem with great wealth as long as folks still have a clue about the rest of the world. We have to come out from behind pristine walls sooner or later; and when we do, we're going to have a head-on collision with reality. The kind of reality that begs the question, "What are you going to do about this?"

Peter and John could have glanced at the nearest sundial and said, "Oops! We're almost late for prayer meeting. Beg on, brother!" Instead, they looked straight at him (v. 4). Refreshing, isn't it? I'm not much for looking suffering and poverty straight in the face.

This man had been crippled from birth. He was taken to the temple every day. I'm convinced that his begging had become tragically rote—completely mechanical. Dear One, I want to say something that may seem harsh. Sometimes we decide God is mean because He won't give us what we're begging for. What we don't realize is that He has a higher mercy toward our crippled state. We want a Holy Enabler. God wants to be our Healer.

They Gave What They Had

Third, Peter and John gave what they had. I love the words in the King James Version. "Silver and gold have I none; but such as I have give I thee: In the name of Jesus Christ of Nazareth rise up and walk" (Acts 3:6, KJV). God never asks us to give what we don't have! Somehow I'm relieved by that assurance.

REFLECTION

WHAT DO YOU HAVE TO GIVE? ARE YOU USING IT FAITHFULLY IN CHRIST'S SERVICE?

Recently this verse came alive for me. Soon after the terrorist attack on the Twin Towers, clergy and church leadership in New York City found themselves overwhelmed by the task of ministering to their flocks after such unprecedented disaster. The American Association of Christian Counselors was asked to lead a training conference for dealing with grief caused by trauma. The AACC quickly pulled together their most experienced Christian counselors and also asked a handful of Christian speakers to join them. I'm still mystified to have been among those invited.

On my way in the airplane, I poured out my heart to God: "Lord, I'm over my head here. I'm out of my league. I don't know what I'm talking about, and I have nothing in my experience to draw from!" The Holy Spirit reminded me of Acts 3:6. God seemed to say, "Beth, I'm not sending you to New York City as a Christian counselor. Don't try to be what you're not. Go and do what I've taught you to do. Teach My Word." Although I was still very intimidated by the task, God's reminder was profound to me. I began my message with this verse. I confessed my tremendous lack of experience and credentials but pledged that such as I have give I thee. I was so relieved not to have to try to be something that I'm not.

Can you relate in any way? If so, how?

Peter Offered His Hand

Fourth, Peter took the beggar by the hand and helped him up. I love this part of the story. Peter and John knew better than anyone that the power to heal the man came solely from the Holy Spirit. The man wasn't healed because Peter took him by the hand and helped him up. Peter offered the man a handful of faith to help him get to his feet. After all, this man had been crippled all his life. What reason did he have to believe he could be healed? All he thought he wanted was a little money. When the beggar grabbed on to Peter's hand, he felt the strength in his grip. The confidence of his faith. In one clasp, Peter offered a handful of faith; and that was all the man needed to come to his feet.

Oh, Beloved, can you see him? Can you see the beggar jumping to his feet, his tin cup tumbling down the temple steps and the few measly coins spinning in the afternoon sunshine? Look at the expression on his face! Watch him dance on legs thin from atrophy. Look! Look straight at him! That's him jumping and praising God through the temple courts.

They Gave Credit to God

Fifth, Peter and John took no credit for the miracle. After all, if man can do it, it really isn't a miracle, is it? Miracles are from God … for the likes of crippled men. Someone reading today has been begging God for trivial things like silver and gold, when God really wants to raise him or her up to jump, dance, and praise Him. Why do we want God to help us stay like we are? Grab a handful of faith and be changed!

❦ Before the Sanhedrin ❦

I love the Book of Acts. In Acts 3, we saw that Peter and John gave the beggar just a handful of faith. That's all it took to bring him to his feet. But because the man could not contain his joy and went leaping about, the two were in trouble. And that's where we pick up, in Acts 4.

Before the Sanhedrin

As Peter and John stood before the chief priests and the guards, verse 13 tells us, "When they saw the courage of Peter and John and realized that they were unschooled, ordinary men, they were astonished and they took note that these men had been with Jesus." Since the priests could see the man who had been healed standing there with them, there was nothing they could say. Read Acts 4:15-22 to see what the Sanhedrin did next. Did you notice in verse 17 that they were afraid to speak the name out loud? Don't you love it? We know that name well. Amen?

The Prayer of the Believers

Now pick up with me in verse 23, because that is the heart of our text. Read Acts 4:23-31 to discover what the believers prayed that was so powerful. Notice that something astonishing happened. After they prayed, the room starting shaking.

Understand that the believers were praying for very specific things. Their prayer was for God to do something. They were asking for God (1) to continue His mighty work—I think especially through Peter and John, (2) to continue to stretch forth His hand and heal through them, and (3) to give them the power to speak boldly. But that's not what God ended up doing. I am convinced that when they got together and prayed over Peter and John, their intent was to pray just for those two. The point that I'm making is that they asked for one very specific thing and got entirely another.

How did God respond, and why in the world do you think He responded as He did?

First of all, look what happened as the result of their prayer. The place where they were meeting was shaken. God came to that place, and He rocked that house, amen? That's the kind of environment I occasionally want to be in. I've asked God to show me His glory, but only as much of His glory as He can without killing me.

Second, they were all filled with the Holy Spirit. He shook the whole house. Not one of them missed it! Then He gave them all the ability to speak the Word of God boldly. We're talking a confidence to share the Word, here, not meanness.

Beloved, God wants to pour out His Holy Spirit on you. He wants to fill your mouth with His Word so that you can speak it with confidence. God looks in the pew at that person who feels as insignificant as could possibly be and He says, "You are the one I would be so willing to pour My Spirit upon. Would you desire that?"

KEY SCRIPTURE

ON THEIR RELEASE, PETER AND JOHN WENT BACK TO THEIR OWN PEOPLE AND REPORTED ALL THAT THE CHIEF PRIESTS AND ELDERS HAD SAID TO THEM. WHEN THEY HEARD THIS, THEY RAISED THEIR VOICES TOGETHER IN PRAYER TO GOD. —ACTS 4:23-24

REFLECTION

HAVE YOU ACCEPTED THE FACT THAT GOD CAN USE YOU TO CARRY OUT HIS WILL? WHY OR WHY NOT?

How They Looked to God

What was it in that Acts 4 environment that God approved of so much that He poured out His Spirit so lavishly? I'd like to suggest six points.

1. They neither denied nor minimized the seriousness of their problem.—These people were normal flesh-and-blood people who were inhabited by the Holy Spirit of the living God. They had all the same fears that we have. The smell of crucifixion was still very much in the air. They knew the reality of persecution. "Do not speak this name again." Don't minimize how that must have felt to them. Be impressed with the fact that they went and did it in spite of their fear.

2. The believers united for prayer in a way God highly honors.—The word *together* in verse 24 looks so benign in our English. The definition of the Greek word is "with one mind, with unanimous consent, in one accord all together." In other words, that group of people got together with a common, united passion and mind. God says in Philippians 2:5 that He wants us to be of one mind—Christ's.

3. They corporately exalted God.—In doing so, they glorified God and also reminded themselves of the One to whom they belonged. They acknowledged that He is sovereign. We need that reminder over and over again when our problem is huge. We need to get our eyes off the problem and the size of the problem and begin just praising the virtues of God. Glorifying God builds up our own faith.

4. They cited Scripture relevant to their challenge.—In verses 25 and 26, they began talking about what David said. They drew from Old Testament Scripture a precedent.

Read 2 Timothy 4, verses 16 and 17. The apostle Paul said this. Did you catch his statement? "I was delivered from the lion's mouth."

Paul very possibly could have been in a situation in Rome where he would be handed over to the lions. He drew back to the story of Daniel in the lion's den. He claimed that precedent of God for the situation he found himself in. He may not have been facing the lions. But he was saying that he might as well have his head in a lion's mouth!

5. They reminded themselves that anything God allows to threaten His own, He uses to bring about great glory.—They were reminding themselves of God's sovereignty, that if He allowed a threat to come to His child, it was because there was great glory to be gained, and they trusted in that.

6. They asked big things.—So often we think so little and ask so little, that we get exactly what we ask—so little. They asked big things. But what they got was even bigger. They came together, united in mind. God approved of their approach so much that He blessed them ... every single one of them.

"At my first defense no one came to my support, but everyone deserted me. May it not be held against them, but the Lord stood at my side and gave me strength, so that through me the message might be fully proclaimed and all the Gentiles might hear it. And I was delivered from the lion's mouth." —2 Timothy 4:16-17

In a Samaritan Village

Over the next several chapters in the Book of Acts, persecution increased like stones pummeled from the hands of a crazed mob. The reality of the Jewish leaders' intentions rose frighteningly to the surface as Stephen fell to his knees. (See Acts 7:54-60.)

The Spread of the Gospel

Read Acts 8:1-4. What was the result of the persecution?

When Christ told His disciples that they would receive power and become witnesses not only in Jerusalem but to the uttermost parts of the earth, they never expected His means! No, His ways are not our ways. Our ways would always be comfortable. Convenient. Certainly without harm.

Read Acts 8:4-25, giving attention to John's appearance in the scene. Where did the apostles in Jerusalem send Peter and John and why?

The Gospel Overcame Prejudice

Does Samaria and its relationship to John ring a bell of any kind to you? The first bell this reference probably rings is the word Christ spoke over the eleven disciples in Acts 1:8 before His ascension. I'd like to suggest that when Christ made the proposal that His disciples would be witnesses in Samaria, He raised a few eyebrows. Jerusalem? No problem. Judea? Absolutely. Ends of the earth? We're Your men, Jesus. But Samaria? Jews despised the Samaritans!

Take a good look at Luke 9:51-56. You can easily see the ill feelings on both sides; however, get a load of our friends James and John. What did they suggest in verse 54?

Jesus took great offense to their suggestion. The gospel had not reached the Samaritans yet. Those who had died would have perished in their sins. Believers often charge the lost with not taking hell seriously enough, but I'm not sure we take it very seriously ourselves. To hope someone "burns in hell" is profoundly offensive to God and proves we lack His heart. (See Ezek. 33:11 and 2 Pet. 3:9.) James and John didn't volunteer to call fire down from heaven in order to save Jesus the trouble. They wanted the head-trip of wielding that kind of power.

Instead of threatening His childish followers with a dose of their own medicine, Jesus chose a far more effective route. He assigned John to be an ambassador of life to the very people John had volunteered to destroy. Don't think for an instant John's assignment was coincidental. As the words fell from Jesus' lips in Acts 1:8, He may very likely have looked straight at John when He said, "and Samaria."

We are naive if we think followers of Christ are automatically void of prejudices. Whether our preferred prejudices are toward denominations, people of other world religions, colors, or

KEY SCRIPTURE

THEN PETER AND JOHN PLACED THEIR HANDS ON THEM, AND THEY RECEIVED THE HOLY SPIRIT.
—ACTS 8:17

economics, they are usually so deeply ingrained in us that we see them far more readily as the way we are rather than as sin. Prejudice is sin. It is the prejudgment and stereotyping of a group of people. Prejudice destroys. Entire world wars have been fought and multi-millions slain over nothing more than what many would term "harmless" prejudice.

One of God's most redemptive tools for dealing with prejudice is appointing His guilty child to get to know a person from the very group she or he has judged. The most obvious work God did in my life involved a woman from one of those churches that my old church would have considered maniacal and unsound. They did not conclude this from firsthand knowledge, of course. The church simply got dumped into one huge category. I was in my twenties and "accidentally" developed a friendship with her before I knew where she went to church. I fell in love with her heart for God. When I found out, I was stunned. She wasn't crazy. She wasn't a maniac. She wasn't unsound. When my other friends would make fun of people from that church, I couldn't bring myself to join in any more. I learned a very important lesson I hope never to forget. Do we even know the people personally who we stereotype and judge?

They Received the Spirit

Acts 8:15 tells us Peter and John prayed for the Samaritans. Persistent prayer is a prejudice-buster every time if we'll let it be. Then something really amazing happened.

Look at verse 17. What action did Peter and John take with the Samaritans?

Well, well, well. They got their wish after all. They called down fire upon them all right. Our God is a consuming fire, and that day He lit the hearts of Samaritans through the hands of Jews. I want to say something so simple but so profound: How I praise God that we—sinful, selfish, ignorant mortals—can change. John wasn't stuck with his old prejudices. God neither gave up on Him nor overlooked the transgression. Acts 8:25 concludes the segment with Peter and John returning to Jerusalem, preaching the gospel in many Samaritan villages. How like Jesus. He turned John's prejudice into a fiery passion. If we truly pursue intimacy with Christ, change will happen. Praise God, it will happen.

Seeing People as Jesus Sees Them

I'd like to conclude with a look at a fascinating account of a unique healing. Read Mark 8:22-25. What makes this account unusual is that we see an incomplete healing that necessitated a second work of Christ. When asked if he saw anything, the blind man looked up and answered, "I see people; they look like trees walking around." I am convinced that no matter how many Bible studies we attend and no matter how we serve our churches, we have not known the deep healing of Christ and the restoration of our souls until the way we view others has dramatically changed. The real issue is not physical sight but spiritual sight. Until we see everything clearly (v. 25). Just as Christ sees them. Christ didn't see people as trees, walking. The blind man wasn't healed until he saw people as Christ saw them.

Beloved, do we still see people as trees, walking? Do we see them as distortions of who they really are? Are we willing to allow God to change our minds and adjust our sight? We're only half-healed until we are.

Some people brought a blind man and begged Jesus to touch him. He took the blind man by the hand and led him outside the village. When he had spit on the man's eyes and put his hands on him, Jesus asked, "Do you see anything?" He looked up and said, "I see people; they look like trees walking around." Once more Jesus put his hands on the man's eyes. Then his eyes were opened, his sight was restored, and he saw everything clearly.—Mark 8:22-25

In Obscurity

Beginning with chapter 9, the Book of Acts traces almost every move Paul made, while John's ministry continued with very little record. I wonder what the apostles thought about Paul gaining so much of the spotlight. Galatians tells us John was a pillar of the church in Jerusalem, but we hear very little about him after his work among the Samaritans in Acts 8.

John's Ministry in Ephesus

We know John lived in Jerusalem, where he cared for Jesus' mother, Mary, and served as a leader in the church. Most historians and scholars agree that John later moved to Ephesus. Nothing at all is recorded in the Bible about his life in Ephesus. Though we have much information about Paul's ministry there, we know virtually nothing about John's.

Ephesus was near the Aegean coast, and it was a center of commerce in that age. Ancient Ephesus was a center of black magic, and the renowned temple to the goddess Diana was located there. Obviously this was a place where the gospel was urgently needed. Paul spent several crucial years ministering in Ephesus, and God performed many supernatural acts there through him. John? He probably lived there shortly after Paul, serving in biblical obscurity.

Tested Over Time

John outlived all the other disciples, who were all counted worthy to give their lives for the sake of Christ. Do you think he ever felt unimportant? If he did struggle with his identity in the era of the early church, he must have chosen to believe what he knew rather than what he felt. We know because of the spiritual fruit produced after years of relative obscurity. In spite of others seeming more powerfully used by God and in the midst of decades hidden in the shadows, John remained persistent in his task. No doubt remains in my mind that God spent this time testing and proving John's character so that he could be trusted with revelation.

I don't think John was so unlike Abraham or Moses. God chose these men but refined them through time to prepare them for their tasks. In terms of John's writings, the earlier and later works were separated by critical years of further preparation.

Months, then years, then even decades may have blown off the calendar of John's life in biblical obscurity; but don't consider for an instant that they were spent in inactivity or emptiness. No possible way! Please do not miss the following point because it is critical: During the interim years of biblical obscurity in John's life, one of the most intense relationships in the entire Word of God developed.

Yes, Christ used John to cast out demons, heal the sick, and spread the good news through word of mouth. But along the way, God built a man to whom He could entrust some of the most profound words ever recorded on parchment. What kind of man writes, "In the beginning was the Word, and the Word was with God, and the Word was God"? Who else could have been entrusted with the love letters of 1, 2, and 3 John? And who in the world could ever be chosen for the penning of the incomparable Revelation? Yet all were indeed entrusted to a man once simply known as "the brother of James."

KEY SCRIPTURE

JAMES, PETER AND JOHN, THOSE REPUTED TO BE PILLARS, GAVE ME AND BARNABAS THE RIGHT HAND OF FELLOWSHIP WHEN THEY RECOGNIZED THE GRACE GIVEN TO ME. THEY AGREED THAT WE SHOULD GO TO THE GENTILES, AND THEY TO THE JEWS.
—GALATIANS 2:9

REFLECTION

HAS THERE BEEN A TIME IN YOUR LIFE WHERE YOU SAW GOD WORKING POWERFULLY IN SOMEONE'S LIFE AND WONDERED WHY HE WASN'T WORKING POWERFULLY IN YOURS? IF SO, WERE YOU FAITHFUL IN DEEPENING YOUR RELATIONSHIP WITH GOD?

The Disciple Jesus Loved

No one knows for certain the exact order of John's writings, but most scholars agree the time frame was the A.D. eighties and nineties. If so, decades passed as John the apostle served in places like Jerusalem and Ephesus, while the other disciples were each martyred one by one.

Somewhere in the midst of those years and decades, John formed the identity of the Beloved Disciple. By the time the words of his Gospel were transferred by the Holy Spirit to him, this identity was intact. John alone called himself "the disciple Jesus loved." At first glance we might be tempted to think John a bit arrogant for terming himself such; but God would never allow a man who received such revelation to get away with that kind of self-promotion. I'd like to suggest that John's evolving identity over the course of those years came out of the opposite kind of heart. God is far too faithful not to have greatly humbled John before giving him such surpassing revelation.

> **"Though the mountains be shaken and the hills be removed, yet my unfailing love for you will not be shaken nor my covenant of peace be removed," says the Lord, who has compassion on you.**
> **—Isaiah 54:10**

As the years went by and the virile, youthful fisherman grew old and gray, I am convinced his weakening legs were steadied and strengthened on the path by the constant reassurance, "Jesus, You chose me. You keep me. And above all else, You love me. You love me. No matter what happens or doesn't, Jesus, I am Your beloved." The times I have most identified myself as loved by God have, without exception, been the difficult times. I survived a two-year period of tremendous difficulty by repeating over and over, "Oh, God, I am so thankful I am loved by You. You love me so much. I am Your beloved. The apple of Your eye." Isaiah 54:10 became my absolute lifeline.

> **Satisfy us in the morning with your unfailing love, that we may sing for joy and be glad all our days.—Psalm 90:14**

Psalm 90:14 began my mornings because I couldn't face the day without it. Read this verse. Beloved, you and I are not on love rations!

At this particular point in your life, are you desperate for a surplus of love and acceptance? If so, please try to write why.

Have you already discovered that your need exceeds mortal fulfillment? I've learned the hard way that when I am in a crisis of insecurity or pain, no one has enough of what I need. The attempt to retrieve it from human resources will ultimately result in me despising them and they despising me. God is our only source. He will never resent us for the breadth, depth, and length of our need.

John knew two things, and I believe he grabbed onto them for dear life. He knew he was called to be a disciple. And he knew he was loved. Over the course of time, those two things emerged into one ultimate identity. "I, John, the seed of Zebedee, the son of Salome, the brother of James, the last surviving apostle am he: the one Jesus loves." Beloved disciple. Somewhere along the way, John, that Son of Thunder, forsook ambition for affection. And that, my friend, is why he was sitting pretty when some of the most profound words ever to fall from heaven to earth fell first like liquid grace into his quill.

Chapter Four

A PICTURE OF JESUS

John was determined to show Jesus' absolute deity.

KEY SCRIPTURE

THESE ARE WRITTEN
THAT YOU MAY
BELIEVE THAT JESUS
IS THE CHRIST,
THE SON OF GOD, AND
THAT BY BELIEVING
YOU MAY HAVE LIFE
IN HIS NAME.
—JOHN 20:31

The Purpose of John's Gospel

While Matthew's and Luke's Gospels begin with human genealogies, John's Gospel begins with the proclamation of Jesus Christ, the preexistent, eternal Word. Like several other New Testament books, the end of this Gospel explains the reason why the book had a beginning. Knowing John could say more than the scrolls on earth could record (John 21:25), what caused him to choose the particular accounts recorded in his Gospel? He provides the answer in John 20:31.

John's Purpose

No other Gospel writer surpasses John's determination to express Jesus' absolute deity. John wrote his Gospel so that the reader would behold truth from an utterly convinced eyewitness that Jesus Christ is the uncontested Christ. The Messiah. The Son of God.

Yet to all who received him, to those who believed in his name, he gave the right to become children of God.—John 1:12

Why is this belief so important according to John 1:12?

John knew salvation could not be secured by those who did not acknowledge Jesus Christ as the absolute Son of God. He made sure no one could miss the saving facts in his Gospel. Of course, the reader could see the facts and yet still miss the salvation because something vital is required of anyone who desires to become a child of God: belief! John's primary purpose in writing appears to be to convince his readers to place their trust in Jesus Christ.

Blessings from Christ

Read John 1:14-16 carefully. Write in the space below the overriding concept of these verses. If you will receive what these verses are saying to you, your entire life experience with Jesus will transform.

From the fullness of Jesus' grace, we all receive one _____ after another.

The original word for blessing is *charis*. *Charis* means "grace, particularly that which causes joy, pleasure, gratification, favor, acceptance, ...the free expression of the loving kindness of God to men finding its only motive in the bounty and benevolence of the Giver; unearned and unmerited favor."[1]

Based on John 1:14,16 and this definition, I believe we can accurately draw the following conclusions:

1. Jesus is full of grace and truth; and He's the only One, besides the Father, who is.

2. All of us get to receive from His fullness! Not just John the apostle. Not just Paul, the apostle to the Gentiles. Jesus is full and overflowing with everything any of us who believes could possibly need or desire!

3. These grace gifts flowing from Christ's fullness not only are beneficial but also are expressions of God's favor that cause joy and pleasure!

A Christian Hedonist

It's high time I made a blatant confession. I am a Christian hedonist. Have been for years, even before I knew what the term meant. Jesus makes me happy! He is the uncontested delight of my life. I never intended for this to happen. I didn't even know it was possible. It all started with an in-depth study of His Word, then surged oddly enough with a near emotional and mental collapse. At the end of myself, I came to the beginning of an intensity of relationship with an invisible Savior that no one had ever told me existed. In crude terms, I think He's a blast.

While still in the closet, I began stumbling on other Christian hedonists. Augustine is a good historical example. Of his conversion in A.D. 386 Augustine wrote, "How sweet all at once it was for me to be rid of those fruitless joys which I had once feared to lose!"[2] C.S. Lewis was another. In *The Weight of His Glory* he wrote, "If we consider the unblushing promises of reward and the staggering nature of the rewards promised in the Gospels, it would seem that our Lord finds our desires not too strong, but too weak. We are half-hearted creatures, fooling about with drink and sex and ambition when infinite joy is offered us, like an ignorant child who wants to go on making mud pies in a slum because he cannot imagine what is meant by the offer of a holiday at the sea. We are far too easily pleased."[3]

Don't get me wrong. I'm not saying our motive for pursuing God is strictly for our own delight and satisfaction. We pursue Him because He is the essence of all existence, and His glory is the sole purpose for our creation. (See Isa. 43:7.) However, when we pursue Him and desire to love Him passionately, we will have an unexpected, stunning collision with joy and fulfillment.

Abundant Life

Many inspired men in Scripture confessed the glorious gain of pursuing God, but few can compete with our very own apostle John. In comparing his Gospel with the three Synoptics (the Books of Matthew, Mark, and Luke), John has more to say about the concepts of life, light, love, truth, glory, signs, and belief than anyone else in the entire New Testament. In length of life and depth of love, John discovered the concept of "more." I am convinced a nutshell explanation for John's entire experience and perspective is intimated in one of the most profound statements of Christ ever dictated to John in John 10:10.

I have come that they might have life, and have it _____.

Do you realize, Dear One, that Christ wants you to have a great life? Don't confuse great with no challenges, hardships, or even suffering. In fact, the greatest parts of my life experience have been overcoming the overwhelming in the power of the Holy Spirit. Christian hedonists don't discount suffering. They just don't give up until they find the gain in the loss. (See Phil. 3:8.) At the end of our lives, God wants us to be able to say we lived them fully and we didn't miss a thing He had for us. We had a blast with God. Just like John.

C.S. Lewis was right. We have been too easily pleased. Somewhere along the way, many of us formed a concept of Christ and settled with it. As a result, hearts become accidents waiting to happen; for our souls were created to exult and dance in holy passion. If we don't find it in the Holy One, we'll search for it amid the smoldering heaps of the unholy. I have burn scars to prove it.

Who Is Your Jesus?

Through our study God is calling you and me to believe Him more. John's Gospel doesn't just call us to belief as if past tense and complete. In Christ we are called to be living verbs, Beloved! We are called to the ongoing act of believing! We want to keep believing what Jesus says about Himself, His Father, and us until we meet Him face-to-face.

I'm going to ask you a hard question: Who is your Jesus? Throughout the weeks to come we'll study John's Jesus, full of grace and truth, who offers us one blessing after another. But at this present time, who do we believe Jesus to be with our own lives? In reality, what we believe is measured by what we live. Not by what we say.

If your life were a Gospel like John's, who would people "believe" your Jesus to be? Think specifically and concretely.

The Jesus Who Performs Miracles

I derived most of my early impressions about Jesus based not so much on what I learned at church but what I saw at church. I certainly believed Jesus saves, and that belief led me to my own salvation experience. But, I believed Him for little more because I saw evidence of little more.

John went out of his way to present us an all-powerful Son of God who speaks and His Word is accomplished. A Savior who not only saves us from our sins but also can deliver us from evil. A Great Physician who really can heal, and a God of glory who reveals His magnificence to mere mortals. And yes, a God of signs and wonders. We've already seen John write that one of his chief purposes in his Gospel was to testify to the signs Jesus performed so readers would believe—not in the miracles themselves, but in the Christ who performed them.

> Jesus Christ is the same yesterday and today and forever.
> —Hebrews 13:8

God may employ miracles less frequently these days, but I know Jesus Christ still performs miracles. I know He does based on Hebrews 13:8. Read this verse. What can we conclude about the Jesus of the Gospels and the Jesus of the twenty-first century?

The second reason I know Jesus Christ still performs miracles is because I am one of them. I was in the clutches of a real, live devil, living in a perpetual cycle of defeat. Only a miracle-working God could have set me free then dared to use me.

Third, I know Jesus Christ still performs miracles because I've witnessed them. Jesus healed a woman I know personally from liver cancer and a man I know personally from pancreatic cancer. I've seen women bear healthy children who were diagnosed inside the womb with debilitating conditions. I was in a service with a dear friend who had been legally blind for years when God suddenly restored a remarkable measure of his sight. Right on the pew of a Baptist church! Hallelujah!

Student of God's Word, the Jesus of some of our churches, denominations, family, and friends may not be able to deliver us, heal us, and stun us with amazing feats; but the Jesus of Scripture can. And He's the same yesterday and today and forever. It's time we started believing Him for more. When we've turned the last page of this Bible study, may we be found firmly embracing the powerful and believable Jesus of God's Word.

🌴 Performer of Miracles 🌴

Jesus loves weddings. There's no doubt about it. The preexistent Eternal Word began His divine thesis with the first one in Genesis 2 and concludes it with the last one in Revelation 19. Please read John 2:1-11.

Jesus Loved Parties

We can readily assume the families involved in the wedding were people Jesus knew well. The wedding date caught Jesus at a critically busy time, just as His Father was launching Jesus' ministry. For Him to be intentional enough to attend this wedding tells us He had relationships and divine purpose there. The hosts probably were good family friends since Mary obviously helped with the wedding.

I believe Jesus had another reason why He didn't have to have His arm twisted to attend the wedding. I happen to think He loved a good party, and still does. I am convinced Jesus' basic personality in His brief walk in human flesh was delightful and refreshingly relational.

In Matthew 9:14-15, Jesus referred to Himself as the Bridegroom. This passage infers that Jesus in our midst is reason enough to celebrate. Why in the world have we let "partying" become associated with immorality? God created man and formed within him an authentic soul-need to feast and celebrate. In fact, God deemed celebration so vital, He commanded His people to celebrate at frequent intervals throughout the calendar year. (See Lev. 23.) Let me say that again: He commands we celebrate His goodness and His greatness!

I say it's time we take the whole idea of "partying" back. I'm always mystified that many non-believers think Christians must be dull, bored, and wouldn't know a good time if it socked them in the noggin. Boy, do we have a secret! No one laughs like a bunch of Christians! My staff and I roll with laughter together at times. Unbelievers might be insulted to know that when we go to their parties, we wonder why they think they're having such a good time. Lean over here closely so I can whisper: I think they're boring.

Abundant Partying

The primary reason why celebrations around Christ's presence are so wonderful is because they are the kind intended to be sparkling refreshment to a world-worn soul. We get to attend Christ's kinds of parties without taking home a lot of baggage. We don't have a hangover later or a guilty conscience. Christ-centered celebrations are all the fun without all the guilt. That's real partying.

When was the last time you attended a party centered around Christ's presence? Describe it briefly in the margin.

How fitting that the penman who had more to say about abundant life and joyful living than any other Gospel writer was also the only one inspired to tell us about the wedding in Cana, an event where "more" became the very issue at hand. Can't you hear Mary? "They have no more wine. And, Son, You're the only one who can give them what they need. More."

KEY SCRIPTURE

THIS, THE FIRST OF HIS MIRACULOUS SIGNS, JESUS PERFORMED AT CANA IN GALILEE. HE THUS REVEALED HIS GLORY, AND HIS DISCIPLES PUT THEIR FAITH IN HIM. —JOHN 2:11

REFLECTION

WHAT CAUSED YOU TO BEGIN YOUR ADVENTURE WITH CHRIST?

The Impact of the Party

Many scholars believe John was a teenager when he followed Christ. That's a partying age if you'll ever find one! The wedding at Cana had a tremendous impact on him. Look at the last statement in John 2:11 to see how John and the other disciples responded.

It's one thing to follow Christ around the countryside. It's another thing to put your faith in Him. Never lose sight of the fact that Judas followed Jesus. Jesus is looking for true disciples who really place their faith—their trust—in Him. We can follow Jesus to every youth retreat in the nation and follow Him down the aisles of every church in America and never put our faith in Him. John officially began his own great adventure of believing right there in Cana.

Yes, it was a big day for John. It was also a big day on the kingdom calendar. Look again at John 2:11. Any first in Scripture is huge. How Jesus chose to perform His first miracle cannot be overestimated. The scene is replete with more applications than we have space to discuss.

Filling Empty Jars

First of all, God ordained that Christ's first earthbound miracle would be filling empty jars. Praise God! Does any pain rival that of emptiness? Beloved, you can take this one to the spiritual bank: any compulsion for too much of anything is a symptom of the horror and urgency of emptiness. Far too many people think that the "good Christian thing to do" about our gnawing emptiness is get a grip, stop whining, and live without for the rest of our lives. If that's what we do, we miss the very first miracle Jesus came to perform! John's Gospel came along to give us the best of good news. We were never meant to live with emptiness! We were meant to be full—we were all meant to receive His fullness and one blessing after another!

Let me echo a precept underscored continually through this two-week study of John's Gospel. We were created to be full. When we're not filled with the good things Christ came to bring us, we will grasp at anything as a substitute.

Write about an example from your own life that supports this precept.

"No one sews a patch of unshrunk cloth on an old garment, for the patch will pull away from the garment, making the tear worse. Neither do men pour new wine into old wineskins. If they do, the skins will burst, the wine will run out, and the wineskins will be ruined. No, they pour new wine into new wineskins, and both are preserved."—Matthew 9:16-17

**Do not get drunk on wine, which leads to debauchery. Instead, be filled with the Spirit.
—Ephesians 5:18**

New Wine

Second, the first miracle brought new wine. To the woman at the well, He would bring the Living Water. (See John 4:13-14.) To the guests at the wedding, He brought new wine. He gives us what we need.

This miracle performed in the physical realm was meant to reveal something far more glorious in the spiritual realm. Though Jesus certainly met an immediate need at the wedding, the wine represented something of exceeding significance. Read Matthew 9:16-17. Christ was making an analogy between the legalistic religion of the day and the true religion that He came to earth to model. One reason Christ came was to fill the emptiness created by the letter of the law, ritual religion, or any earthly substitute—the "old wine." What was the "new wine"? I believe it is beautifully inferred in Ephesians 5:18.

How does this passage tell us to fill ourselves?

> **Do not get drunk on wine, which leads to debauchery.**
> **Instead, be filled with _____ _____.**

The passage is also inferring that the filling of the Holy Spirit does in full measure what we try to accomplish when we desire to be "drunk with wine." Wine was associated with joy and gladness. One reason why people drink much wine is because it changes the way they feel and the way they behave. So does the new wine, but its effects are always good. Jesus came to bring the new wine of the Spirit! This is something we can drink to our fill without all the negative side effects of wine and the emptiness it leaves behind in the wake of the temporary "fix."

Fully Satisfied

At the first revelation of Christ's glory in Cana, the wedding guests had no idea that the true New Wine was on its way! The Master of our banquet saved the best of the wine for last. (See John 2:10.) Beloved, did you realize that among the many gifts and services Christ brought His Holy Spirit to grant, one of them is joy and gladness? Check it out for yourself.

In the margin, finish the list of the "side effects" of this New Wine according to Galatians 5:22-23.

Just think! The more you drink of His Spirit, the more fully satisfied you are with all sorts of side effects we're so desperate to achieve. To top off the goblet, instead of losing self-control, we gain it. You can't beat a drink like that!

When my daughter Melissa was a toddler, she was never satisfied with a little of anything. Every time I offered her a treat, she'd cup her plump little hand, thrust it forward, and say, "Can my have a bawnch (bunch) of it?" The way she saw life, why bother if you can't have a bunch of it? Indeed! John would agree! Dear One, how tragic for us to continue with pangs of emptiness. What a waste! Christ came to bring us a bawnch of joy! Stop feeling guilty because you crave lots of joy in your life. You were made for joy! You are a jar of clay just waiting to be filled. (See 2 Cor. 4:7.) May this lesson end with the clink of our cups as we toast to a life overflowing with New Wine!

The fruit of the Spirit is...
love
joy
peace

_____
_____
_____
_____
_____
_____

—Galatians 5:22-23

We have this treasure in jars of clay to show that this all-surpassing power is from God and not from us.—2 Corinthians 4:7

🦂 Rescuer of the World 🦂

God inspired John to tell us about "the world." While Matthew mentions the world 10 times, Mark mentions it 5 times, and Luke mentions it 7 times, the Gospel of John mentions it a whopping 73 times!

"GOD SO LOVED THE WORLD THAT HE GAVE HIS ONE AND ONLY SON, THAT WHOEVER BELIEVES IN HIM SHALL NOT PERISH BUT HAVE ETERNAL LIFE."—JOHN 3:16

Following are a few Scriptures in John's Gospel that contain the word *world*. **Look up every single one and note beside each reference what the Holy Spirit inspired John to make sure we knew about the world.**

John 1:10

John 1:29

John 3:16

John 3:17

John 3:19

The Creation of the World

Perhaps the most overwhelming fact of all these verses is one to which we've grown inordinately casual: Jesus was sent by God to the world. I hope you didn't miss that the Father and Son had fellowship and shared glory before the world even existed. In fact, mankind exists out of the holy passion of the Trinity to draw others into their fellowship.

The Father, Son, and Holy Spirit, complete in themselves, desired the exceeding joy of additional relationship; so "in the beginning God created the heavens and the earth" (Gen. 1:1). Although distinctions exist between the words *earth* and *world,* they are intertwined and virtually interchangeable where creation is concerned. Genesis 1:1 tells us that God created the earth, and John 1:10 tells us the world was made through Jesus. "Earth" tends to encompass the physical properties of our planet while "world" encases more of the system, social and otherwise, on it. You might think of the distinction this way: Our world is on this earth.

God the Father, Son, and Holy Spirit desired the existence of man so they could have fellowship with man. They wanted him to have a will of his own because they wanted to be chosen. Not commanded. They knew that equipping him with a will of his own would necessitate a plan for redemption because he would ultimately make some very poor choices. Thus, the plan of salvation was already completely intact before the creation of the world. When the Holy Trinity was ready, each member participated in the astonishing six-day creation.

One Tiny Planet

Our solar system is in a galaxy called the Milky Way. There are about 100 billion stars in the Milky Way. Scientists estimate that there are more than 100 billion galaxies scattered throughout the visible universe.

Impressive, isn't it? But this gets even more impressive: In the beginning God created the sun, the moon, every single star, all their surrounding planets … and the earth. You and I have no idea what God's activities may have been elsewhere in the universe; but according to the Bible and as far as He wanted us to know, He picked out one tiny speck upon which to build a world. Our world. And He picked it out so that when the time had fully come, He could send His Son. (See Gal. 4:4.) Can you imagine the fellowship of the Trinity on the seventh day? As they rested and looked upon the very good work they had accomplished, one planet had been tended like no other to our knowledge. Perfectly placed in the universe with adequate distance from sun, moon, and stars to sustain human life, it was chosen for divine infiltration.

Why in heaven's name did God single out one tiny planet to so love? Beloved, absorb this into the marrow: because we are on it. As unlovable as humanity can be, God loves us. We are His treasures. His prize creation. He can't help it. He just loves us. So much in fact that He did something I with my comparatively pitiful love for my children would not do for anyone.

God's Vast Love

Dear One, let it fall afresh. I am overcome with emotion. Elohim is so huge. We are so small. Yet the vastness of His love—so high, so wide, so deep, so long—envelopes us like the endless universe envelopes a crude little planet God first called "earth."

Not long ago, my husband, Keith, had a bench placed in the corner of our backyard. Almost every morning, I light a candle and head out to that bench for a pre-dawn worship service and quiet time. Sometimes I have to pull a big blanket out of a warm dryer to wrap around me in the cold. At that time in the morning, the heavens are still as dark as the blackest night, and the stars look like God lit ten thousand candles of His own. In that morning hour, I feel like He lit them just for the two of us. David the psalmist was besieged by the sight. Read Psalm 8:3-4.

In the midst of constant discoveries, modern science hasn't even begun to discover the true wonder of God's universe; yet even when I consider what they do know, I am overwhelmed with David's same question: Who are we, God of all creation, that You would give a single thought to us? Let alone a mindful.

My daughter Amanda was a dreamy, tenderhearted toddler. I often stooped down to talk to her so that I could look her right in those big, blue-green eyes. Every time I squatted down to talk to her, she squatted down too … and there we'd be. The gesture was so precious I always had to fight the urge to laugh. I dared not because she was often very serious.

The psalmist wrote "Your right hand sustains me; you stoop down to make me great" (Ps. 18:35). I don't think the Scripture applies to us in the modern world's understanding of greatness. I think it says to us, "You stoop down and make me significant." When the God of all the universe stoops down and a single child recognizes the tender condescension and bends his or her knees to stoop as well, the heart of God surges with unbridled emotion.

As you conclude, read John 1:10-12 with all this in mind, aloud and thoughtfully. Much of the world carries on as if their Creator did not exist. Oh, but He does. Bow down, dear children of God. His love has made you significant.

REFLECTION

HOW HAVE YOU EXPERIENCED GOD'S LOVE THIS WEEK?

When I consider your heavens, the work of your fingers, the moon and the stars, which you have set in place, what is man that you are mindful of him, the son of man that you care for him?

—Psalm 8:3-4

The Great "I Am"

Today we are going to take an overall look at seven claims Christ made about who He is. These seven titles by no means are the totality of His claims. They simply share several common denominators in John's Gospel that we don't want to miss. The Gospel of John tells us more about the self-proclaimed identity of Christ than the others.

Look up each reference below and note Christ's claims of identity in the space provided.

John 6:35: I AM the _____

John 8:12: I AM the _____

John 10:7-9: I AM the _____

John 10:11-14: I AM the _____

John 11:25: I AM the _____

John 14:6: I AM the _____

John 15:1,5: I AM the _____

I see three basic common denominators in these seven titles. Consider each with me.

1. All seven titles are preceded by "I am." Consider the impact of these two words coming from the mouth of Jesus Christ. Read John 8:48-59. Now meditate on the power-packed claim of Christ in John 8:58.

How did the Jews react to Christ's statement?
___ They tried to stone Him.   ___ They ran after Him.   ___ They ran from Him.

The reason why they reacted so violently was because they knew exactly what Christ was inferring. They wanted to stone Him for blasphemy because they understood His reference to God's introduction of Himself to Moses in Exodus 3:12-15. Read Exodus 3:14.

One of God's primary points to Moses is stated in Exodus 3:12: "I will be with you." This Great I Am that I Am introduced Himself by this title in context with the promise to be with man. He did not need them. Rather, they needed Him; and He came in response to that need. The Jews listening to Christ in John 8 knew exactly what Christ meant by His "I Am!" statement. He was claiming to be part of the godhead. Dear Ones, we must consider His claims as well. Either Jesus came as the Incarnate Great I Am or He is a liar. He cannot be anything in between. When Christ says the words "I am," they are falling from the lips of Him who is the Great I Am!

2. The word the is included in each title. Go back and read each of the titles you supplied in your first interactive exercise, but this time substitute the word *the* with the word *a*. What dif-

KEY SCRIPTURE

"I TELL YOU THE TRUTH," JESUS ANSWERED, "BEFORE ABRAHAM WAS BORN, I AM!"—JOHN 8:58

God said to Moses, "I Am Who I Am. This is what you are to say to the Israelites: 'I Am has sent me to you.' "—Exodus 3:14

ference does *the* make? The question may seem elementary scholastically, but nothing could be more profound theologically. For just a moment forget everyone else in the Body of Christ and just think about your own approach to Jesus Christ. Is He *a* light to you or *the* Light? Is He *a* way for you to follow—perhaps here and there in life—or is He *the* way you want to go? Is He *a* means to afterlife in your opinion? In other words, deep down inside do you think that several world religions offer a viable way to life after death, with Jesus just one of them? Or is He *the* resurrection and the life?

3. **Each of the seven "I Am" statements is relational!** Look up all seven titles one more time, but this time look for how the title is associated with man and record them beside the title on the previous page. In other words, find us in the statements. Don't quit on me now! This point is important, and I think you'll receive a blessing. I've given you the first one so you'll understand what I'm asking.

John 6:35: I am the bread of life. He who comes to me will never go hungry.

Jesus Christ is everything we need. Every single one of these titles is for us! Remember, He is the self-sufficient One! He came to be what we need. And not just what we need, but what we desire most in all of life. The "I Am" came to be "with us." I could weep with joy!

We will never have a challenge He's not equipped to empower us to meet. We will never have a need He cannot fill. We will never have an earthly desire He cannot exceed. When we allow Christ to be all He is to us, we find wholeness. One piece at a time, Beloved. Every time you discover the reality of Christ fulfilling another realm of your needs and longings, His Name is written on a different part of you, and you are that much closer to wholeness.

REFLECTION

IS CHRIST AN "A" AMONG SEVERAL OTHER POSSIBILITIES IN THIS LIFE OR IS HE YOUR "THE"?

JESUS ANSWERED, "I AM THE WAY AND THE TRUTH AND THE LIFE. NO ONE COMES TO THE FATHER EXCEPT THROUGH ME." —JOHN 14:6

I tell you the truth, no one can enter the kingdom of God unless he is born of water and the Spirit. Flesh gives birth to flesh, but the Spirit gives birth to spirit.

—John 3:5-6

I tell you the truth, everyone who sins is a slave to sin.... So if the Son sets you free, you will be free indeed.

—John 8:34,36

⤚ Jesus, the Truth ⤙

What is truth? Pilate asked that very question in John 18:38. Ironically, as Pilate acted as though truth were illusive, he was looking into the very face of it. Christ is the truth.

I Tell You the Truth

Perhaps all of us have been hurt and betrayed by some kind of lie. Beloved, Christ will not, and indeed, cannot deceive you. He will always tell us the truth, even when it's hard to hear. Today, let's allow these words of Christ to fall afresh on our injured hearts: "I tell you the truth."

Read John 3:5-6. Was Christ capable of telling anything but the truth? Absolutely not! Yet in 77 instances in the Bible (NIV), he began explaining a certain principle by saying, "I tell you the truth." John was adamant that we understood the importance of and the role of truth. I'm going to cite three reasons why I believe John emphasized truth in his Gospel.

First of all, Christ began a statement with "I tell you the truth" just for the sake of emphasis. Every single time you see that phrase in Scripture, take another look at the verse. There's something He is emphasizing.

Second, He used the phrase for clarity on issues of profound importance like life and death. We've just read one matter of profound importance. Right there in John 3:5 He was telling us how we must be born again. "Verily, verily, I say unto thee." (KJV) "I tell you the truth." In other words, listen carefully. He was giving us a prescription for salvation, and He didn't want us to miss it.

Third, He used the phrase to clarify issues of controversy. He drew a line, a dividing line. He often began a concept by saying, in effect: I am telling you the truth. If you'll listen to me, you'll know which side of this line to get on.

Feel-Good Scripture

Some of Christ's "I tell you the truth" statements really make us feel good. They are good feel-good Scriptures; and we can know they are the truth!

Read the following verses and write what they say to you.

John 14:12:

John 16:23:

Jesus will also tell us the truth about things that confront us. Read John 8:34,36. He was saying: Frankly, I'm just going to tell you something. You are a slave to this stuff until I come and set you free.

Confrontational Scripture

So there are times that Jesus began a confrontational statement by saying, "I'm going to tell you the truth." Some confrontational statements might upset us. Let me give you a perfect example. Peter would know this one by heart. John overheard it. But neither would have talked about it much. Read John 21:18.

It was true. It was something that Christ meant to emphasize. It was a matter of life and death, as Peter would find out. It was emphasized by the words "I tell you the truth." Some make us feel wonderful, some confront us, and still others might upset us.

Truth Breeds Trust

I believe, above all things, that truth breeds trust. I want you to look at that again. TRUTH BREEDS TRUST. I believe that truth breeds more trust than even love. I have had people in my life that really could tell me honestly that they loved me. However, they were unhealthy enough to have betrayed my trust by telling me things that I could not believe, when all was said and done.

Sadly, because we are people of this world, we also have betrayed others. We've all been betrayed; we have all betrayed others in one form or another. We've all known what it's been like to hear someone say, "But I love you." And every once in a while we just want to say, "You know what? Save it and tell me the truth. Then we'll work on love." I like to do truth first. Trust is everything to me.

To me, relationships are built on trust. And to me, it is truth that breeds that kind of trust. You may have experienced unhealthy love. You may have loved someone with unhealthy love. That's why, Beloved, the Word of God says that we are to love Him first and then love others. That love has got to go vertical (to God) before it goes horizontal (to people). When I love Him first, it is as if He is able to take some of the toxins and poisons out of my human love, my natural love, before it goes horizontal. It's as if Christ says to us: Put your chief affections on me, then I will help you be the kind of person that could love other people in a healthy way.

A question you have to ask yourself over and over again is "Has Jesus told me the truth?" Why? Because, as John 8:32 tells us, only the truth sets us free. So here's the real question that is pivotal in your journey: Do you trust God? Because it comes down to that over and over again: Do you trust Me, child?

"I tell you the truth, when you were younger you dressed yourself and you went where you wanted; but when you are old you will stretch out your hands, and someone else will dress you and lead you where you do not want to go." —John 21:18

REFLECTION

ARE ANY OF YOUR LOVE RELATIONSHIPS BUILT ON UNHEALTHY LOVE? ARE YOUR RELATIONSHIPS BUILT ON LOVE FOR GOD FIRST, THEN LOVE FOR OTHERS?

1. Spiros Zodhiates, *The Complete Word Study Dictionary: New Testament* (Chattanooga, TN: AMG Publishers, 1992), 1469.
2. Augustine, *Confessions,* trans. R. S. Pine-Coffin (New York: Penguin Books, 1961), 181 (IX, 1).
3. C. S. Lewis, *The Weight of His Glory and Other Addresses,* (Grand Rapids, Mich.: Eerdmans, 1965), 1-2.

Chapter Five
THE ABUNDANT LIFE

The Holy Spirit is the key to the abundant life God wants for us.

KEY SCRIPTURE

THE COUNSELOR,
THE HOLY SPIRIT,
WHOM THE FATHER
WILL SEND IN MY
NAME, WILL TEACH
YOU ALL THINGS AND
WILL REMIND YOU OF
EVERYTHING I HAVE
SAID TO YOU.
—JOHN 14:26

More of the Holy Spirit

This week we will emphasize the concepts of "more" and "abundance" tucked like priceless treasures in John's Gospel. John gives us more information about the Holy Spirit than any other Gospel writer. The Holy Spirit (*He*, not *It*) is the focus of today's study. I wish I could write the next statement in neon lights upon this page to catch the eye of every reader: The Holy Spirit is the key to everything in the life of the believer in Christ!

Vital Keys to Victorious Life

I received so many wonderful treasures from the churches of my youth, but I did not learn two of the most vital keys to a victorious life: how to have an ongoing, vibrant relationship with God through His Word, and how to be filled with the power and life of the Holy Spirit. Both of these are vital concepts that the enemy (Satan) does everything he can to ensure we miss. The Word and the Holy Spirit are by far Satan's biggest threats. I don't think John would mind if his contemporary, Paul, launched our study today. Read 1 Corinthians 2:9-14, looking for the reason the Holy Spirit is so vital in a relationship with God through His Word. Beloved, whether or not you start reaping the benefits the Holy Spirit came to bring you is up to you!

Now we'll let John tell us what many of those benefits and activities are. John's primary truths on the Holy Spirit are compacted in chapters 14 and 16 of his Gospel. Read both chapters thoroughly and then list pertinent truths recorded about the Holy Spirit.
John 14   John 16

The Spirit Will Be in You

One of the most revolutionary truths Christ told His disciples is in John 14:17. He told them that the Spirit of Truth at that time was living with them but would soon be in them. Think about the difference the Spirit of God could make living in a person as opposed to living with a person. Beloved, that very difference turned a band of fumbling, fleshly followers into sticks of spiritual dynamite that exploded victoriously on the world scene in the Books of Acts. The difference is enormous! It would be impossible to overestimate!

The fulfillment of Christ's promise to His disciples came to them in Acts 2:1-4. These glorious events unleashed the Holy Spirit for the "Church Age" and onward until the return of Christ. The Holy Spirit now indwells every person who receives Christ as his or her personal Savior. (See Rom. 8:9.) Oh, that we would absorb the magnitude of this spiritual revolution! Dear believer in Christ, the Spirit of the Living God—the Spirit of Jesus Christ Himself, the Spirit of Truth—dwells inside of you!

Oh, Beloved, I hope you are "getting" this. I am about to hop out of my chair. I can barely type! You and I need nothing on this earth like a continual filling of the Holy Spirit. Do we need extra patience? Could we use a little peace in the midst of chaos? Do we need to show an extra measure of kindness? How about a heaping helping of joy? Remember Galatians 5:22-23? All these traits come with the fullness of the Holy Spirit! You see, we don't just need more patience. We need the Holy Spirit filling us and anointing us!

Does anyone need deep insight from God's Word? An added measure of understanding? Does anyone want to fulfill God's eternal purposes for his or her life? All of these come with a filling of the Holy Spirit! (See 1 Cor. 2.) Could anyone use a sharper memory? Beloved, I could! Take another look at John 14:26. The Holy Spirit is the Blessed Reminder. He is your key to memorizing Scripture or retaining anything biblical. Take Him up on it!

REFLECTION

WHAT DO YOU NEED MOST FROM THE HOLY SPIRIT BASED ON THE ACTIVITIES WE'VE CONSIDERED TODAY?

If you then, though you are evil, know how to give good gifts to your children, how much more will your Father in heaven give the Holy Spirit to those who ask him!—Luke 11:13

When you ask, you do not receive, because you ask with wrong motives, that you may spend what you get on your pleasures.
—James 4:3

Let your light shine before men, that they may see your good deeds and praise your Father in heaven.—Matthew 5:16

Seeking More of the Spirit

Are you actively praying for more of Him? Luke 11:11-13 gives us permission to request a filling of the Holy Spirit in our lives. One reason we may not have experienced the fullness of God's presence and empowerment in our lives is that we haven't asked.

James 4:3 adds an additional reason why we don't receive. Sometimes we ask with wrong motives. If I want to be filled with the Holy Spirit so that people will be impressed with me or so that I will "feel" powerful, then my motives are self-glorifying and dishonor God. If I desire the Holy Spirit to work supernaturally as proof that God exists, then my motive is to prove (test) God rather than glorify God. A right motive for asking to be filled with the Holy Spirit is that God be glorified through our effective and abundant Spirit-filled life. Matthew said it best in Matthew 5:16.

God is most glorified in us when we are most satisfied in Him. I don't just want to do the church thing. I want to experience Him every day of my mortal life! I want to bask in the favor of His pure presence. I want God … and a lot of Him! I think you do, too. Let's start asking for Him, Dear One, every day of our lives. More of Your Spirit, Lord. More of Your Spirit!

KEY SCRIPTURE

THIS IS TO MY FATHER'S GLORY, THAT YOU BEAR MUCH FRUIT, SHOWING YOURSELVES TO BE MY DISCIPLES.
—JOHN 15:8

🌴 More Fruit 🌴

I am so overwhelmed by all the Word has to say to us today that I am nearly paralyzed. Read John 15:1-17.

Quite possibly Christ's teaching on the vine took place as He and His disciples walked through a vineyard on their way to the olive grove. I want you to place yourself in this scene. As a follower of Christ, you are a chosen disciple in this generation.

Three sets of "players" are cast in this vineyard allegory. The labels and responsibilities of each one are vital. Note everything you reap from these 17 verses about them.

CHRIST'S FATHER (Gardener)	CHRIST (Vine)	HIS DISCIPLES (Branches)

You Should Bear Much Fruit

What I'm about to say is not to your pastor, your teacher, your mentor, your hero in the faith, or your best friend at church. It's to you. Beloved, the God of all the universe has ordained that your precious life bear much fruit. Do you hear what I'm saying? Are you taking it personally?

This is about God, Christ, and you. Their eyes are on you this very moment. Hear them speak these words into your spirit loud and clear: We want you to bear MUCH fruit.

This week we're talking about more. Today we're going to talk specifically about much. God hasn't appointed you to mediocrity, but to a life of profound harvest. I am sick of the enemy's subtle scheme to convince the masses in the Body of Christ that only a few lives in each generation are truly significant. Your life was set apart for significance! Get up right this second, look in the nearest mirror, and say it out loud to that image in front of you. And while you're at it say, "God has chosen you, and He wants to be glorified by you bearing MUCH fruit." I'm not saying another word until you go to that mirror.

What kinds of things hold us back from bearing much fruit? Give this question some thought.

Past Sins

I hope we clear a few obstacles out of the way through the course of our lesson, but I'd like to address one right away. Many think that the sins of their past have exempted them from tremendously fruit-bearing lives. First of all, if that were true, I assure you I would not be writing to you right now. Second, if we haven't repented and allowed God to restore us and redeem our failures, we will tragically fulfill some of our own self-destructive prophecies. God is not the one holding us back from much fruit after failure. In tandem with the devil, we are the ones. God's primary concern is that He is glorified. Few unmistakable evidences glorify Him more than powerfully restored lives that humbly and authentically proclaim His faithfulness to the death.

God's Promises

The Father is so adamant that we bear much fruit, He has extended amazing offers to us. Allow me to share them with you.

1. He gives us a love we can live in.–When will we get through our heads how loved we are? Take a look at perhaps the most astounding verse in this entire segment of Scripture.

In what way does Christ love His own according to John 15:9?

> "As the Father has loved me, so have I loved you. Now remain in my love."—John 15:9

Try to grasp this truth as tightly as you can: Christ Jesus loves you like the Father loves Him. He loves you like His only begotten! As if you were the only one! Christ follows His statement with a command: Remain in my love. How do we do such a thing? Let me paraphrase what I think Christ is saying in this passage. Put your name in the blanks:

> My love for you, _____, is perfect, divine, and lavish beyond your imagination and far beyond your soul's cavernous needs. In fact, I love you like My Father loves Me; and I am the only begotten Son and the uncontested apple of His eye. _____, my love for you is as constant as an ever-surging fountain; but you don't always sense it because you move in and out of the

awareness of My presence. My desire is for you to pitch your mobile home so intimately close to me that you are never outside the keen awareness of My extravagant love.

Why is a constant awareness of God's love for us so vital in a profusely fruit-bearing life? One reason is because the last thing Satan wants is for our lives to bear much fruit. He will do everything he can to discourage us, accuse us, and try to condemn us. Even the most steadfast among God's servants make mistakes and foolish decisions of some kind along the way. None is worthy to serve the Holy God of all creation. We will always give Satan plenty of ammunition to discourage us. If we don't literally camp in the love of Christ, we will talk ourselves out of untold fruit by dwelling on our own unworthiness. Let's just accept the fact that we are unworthy and that we're lavishly loved by a God of redemptive grace.

2. He is a source we can draw from.—Earlier when I asked what kinds of things hold us back from immensely fruit-bearing lives, you may have responded "a lack of talent or ability." Conspicuously missing in this unparalleled dissertation on lives bearing much fruit is any reference whatsoever to ability.

In verse 5, Christ told us that all we have to do is embed ourselves in Him and let the power source flow. He does the work through us. That's the secret! I spent the first half of my adult life trying my hardest to make something—anything—work for God. After all, He had called me! Nothing worked … until I gave up in exhaustion and failure and let Him work. We can't force fruit. We can only abide in the Vine. If we're going to produce much fruit, we've got to be open to the life, agenda, and timing of the Vine.

REFLECTION

WHAT KINDS OF THINGS HOLD YOU BACK FROM AN IMMENSELY PRODUCTIVE LIFE?

3. He is a Gardener we can depend on.—You've heard of personal trainers. Our Gardener is so determined that fruitful lives bear even more fruit, He commits Himself as our personal Pruner! Notice verse 2. I believe this verse suggests that God works all the harder on a child producing fruit so she or he will produce even more. If you are a true follower of Jesus Christ, you probably sometimes feel like God is picking on you. Have you ever exclaimed in exasperation, "God never lets me get away with anything"? Have you ever noticed that God extracts from your life meaningless activities that He seems to "put up with" in other believers' lives? That, Dear One, is because you have proved to be a cooperative, fruit-bearing child; and He knows He has a prime branch through whom He can be all the more glorified.

Do you see the progression suggested in verses 2 and 5? God desires for those who bear fruit to bear more fruit and those who bear more fruit to bear much fruit! As nervous as the thought may make us, God can be trusted with a pair of sheers in His hand.

The following exercise is strictly for your benefit and between you and God. Don't let Satan use it to condemn you. To the best of your biblical understanding, based on an abiding sense of God's presence and pleasure as opposed to numbers and notoriety, plot where you think you may presently be in the process represented below.

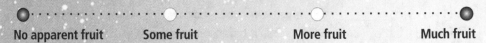

No apparent fruit   Some fruit   More fruit   Much fruit

Abide in Obedience

We will not bear much fruit without obedience to our Father's will. In fact, according to John 15:10, if we don't walk closely to Him in obedience we will never draw near enough to abide in His love. He loves us no matter what we do, but we will not be able to pitch our spiritual tents in His presence when we're disobedient. Does all this sound like a life of just serving and sacrificing? Then you'd better read John 15:11 again.

I have told you this so that my joy may be in you and that your joy may be complete.—John 15:11

What is the result of the obedient, abiding, fruit-bearing life?

Our Heavenly Father is the giver of all good gifts. (See Jas. 1:17.) God longs to bless us with abundant life and joy. Precious One, God doesn't just have more for you. He has much. Much love. Much fruit. Much joy. And the God of the universe derives much glory from one measly mortal. Who can beat a deal like that?

KEY SCRIPTURE

WHOEVER HAS MY
COMMANDS AND
OBEYS THEM, HE IS
THE ONE WHO LOVES
ME. HE WHO LOVES
ME WILL BE LOVED BY
MY FATHER, AND I TOO
WILL LOVE HIM AND
SHOW MYSELF TO HIM.
—JOHN 14:21

🐝 More Revelation 🐝

Read John 14:19-25. In Christ's response to Judas's question, He clearly stated that this particular revealing of Himself would not occur in heaven but on earth. "We will come to him and make our home with him." This statement is in perfect context and beautiful contrast with Christ's promise in John 14:2-3. Christ promised that one day He'd come to take His followers back to be with Him. The assumption is that they (and we) would dwell in the many rooms Christ is preparing. I believe this is what Christ was saying to them: I am going to leave you so that I can prepare rooms for you where you will one day dwell and make yourself at home where I live in heaven. Until then, I have built a room in each of you where I can make Myself at home with you. This way I am at home with you in Spirit until you are at home with Me in heaven.

God Reveals Himself

God and Christ reveal themselves in several different ways. First and foremost, they reveal themselves through the Bible. In fact, Scripture is our only totally reliable source of revelation because it is always true and does not depend on personal opinion.

Scripture is also clear, however, that God reveals dimensions of Himself and His glory to man through other sources. Note those sources from the following references.

Romans 1:20

Acts 14:17

God has never revealed Himself to me in flames of fire from within a bush like He did Moses in Exodus 3:2, nor have I ever seen chariots of fire like Elisha (2 Kings 6:17), but I have often beheld God's glory through nature.

Do you have a favorite place where you've seen God reveal His glory through nature? If so, describe it in the margin.

The Ultimate Revelation of God

God's Word suggests He can reveal Himself in numerous ways; but His ultimate revelation to man was through His very own Son, Jesus. He came to show us God in an embraceable, visible form. I believe a very important part of Christ's promise in John 14:21 is that after His departure, He would continue to reveal, manifest, or make Himself known to His followers here until they were there. Now that His Spirit has come and His Word is complete, I believe they (the Holy Spirit and the Word) are the primary means by which Jesus discloses Himself to His followers.

Conditions for Seeing God

Having built what I pray is a solid theological foundation for Christ's continued revelation to His followers, let's celebrate the enormous ramifications toward our lives. John 14:21 is bulging with conditions to its promises.

1. Love.—Let's immediately diffuse any upset over Christ's statement, "He who loves me will be loved by my Father." Aren't we told in John 3:16 that God so loves the world? Absolutely! Aren't we also told in 1 John 4:19 that we love because He first loved us? No doubt! John 14:21 is not suggesting God's love for us is conditional and responsive to our love for Him. I believe the phrase is best interpreted based on a deeper understanding of the nature of God's love.

Fill in the following blank according to Romans 5:8.
God _____ his own love for us in this: While we were still sinners, Christ died for us.

One of the most significant qualities found in God's brand of love is that it is demonstrative. Christ directed His followers to love as He loved them. We'll look more closely at 1 John 3:18 in our study of John's letters, but notice how this verse directs us to love—with actions.

> **Dear children, let us not love with words or tongue but with actions and in truth.—1 John 3:18**

Do you see the concept? One of the most important dimensions of agape love is that it is demonstrative. I believe John 14:21 is implying that the more we obey and love God, the more vividly we may see, experience, and enjoy demonstrations of His love. This illustration might help.

God brought a darling young woman into my life who had been through untold turmoil. Abused and misused, she didn't trust anyone. She needed love as badly as anyone I had ever known, but she was terribly suspicious and hard to love. God kept insisting that I show her the love of Jesus. One day I said to Him, "Lord, I'm trying to be obedient; but loving her is like trying to hug a porcupine!" Over the months and years, God turned my beloved porcupine into a puppy. I loved her throughout our relationship; but the softer and more loving she became, the more love I was able to show her. On a much greater scale, I believe the principle applies to God's demonstration of love to us.

2. Obedience.—I am convinced John 14:21 suggests that the more we love and obey Christ Jesus, the more He will disclose Himself to us. I am persuaded that the truth God inspired the apostle John to pen in John 14:21 became the man's virtual philosophy and approach to life. We have already concluded that John forsook ambition for affection. Love became his absolute center. As we continue our journey we will also discover that he was a man who pursued obedience even when no one was watching. With his whole being, John lived the divine conditions of John 14:21. Years down the road, is it any wonder our Immortal Savior and Lord hand-picked him when He determined to deliver the incomparable Book of Revelation? How fitting. John himself represents the ultimate human example of his own penmanship.

The Earth Is Full of God's Glory

Isaiah 6:3 tells us the earth is full of God's glory. I believe the glory of our Lord Jesus surrounds us constantly. We are perpetually surrounded by means through which He could show us His worth, His providence, and His presence. We don't want to miss them!

Christ has disclosed Himself to me in my earthly walk in several ways:
• through a Bible teacher or a preacher in such a way that I feel like I'm the only one in the

REFLECTION

HOW HAS CHRIST
SHOWN HIMSELF
TO YOU?

audience and he's read my email.
- when reading a portion of Scripture, suddenly my eyes are opened to an astounding, transforming understanding of Christ.
- at the side of a dying loved one who knows Christ, He manifested such a thickness of His presence that I've been overwhelmed by His care and comfort.
- by working out a problem that no one else knew anything about.
- when an impending disaster is suddenly averted, I've been covered by chills as I've sensed Him as my Deliverer.
- during worship, I've sensed His powerful presence and sweet pleasure.

I've experienced each one of these, but I want to "see" more. I want Jesus Christ to manifest Himself to me! I want to know Him on this earth as well as a mortal can know Him. Don't you? Then let's pray toward that end!

KEY SCRIPTURE

JUST THEN HIS
DISCIPLES RETURNED
AND WERE
SURPRISED TO FIND
HIM TALKING WITH A
WOMAN. —JOHN 4:27

More Interaction with Women

Notice today's Scripture. You might even read it aloud. Do you want to know something? Some of Jesus' followers are still surprised to find Him talking with women. Today's lesson supports the biblical fact that Jesus Christ talks to women … and highly esteems them.

A Woman's Place in God's Heart

The biblical roles and responsibilities of men and women differ sometimes to complement each other. Our places in the heart of God, however, are the same. I am very comfortable in my womanhood in the Body of Christ, but not every woman is. Sometimes a spiritual inferiority complex stems from having been exposed to steady doses of inaccurate representations of Christ and His Word.

My purpose today is to prove an unmistakable tie between several women in the Bible and Christ. Ties, I might add, from which Christ knitted some very deep theology. Yes, Jesus speaks to women who listen. Always has. Always will. Anyone who wants to believe Christ didn't have profound encounters with women might want to skip the Gospel of John. Let me again be clear that the New Testament bulges with encounters and relationships between Christ and men. We're not taking away one iota from those. Our goal today, however, is to study His interaction with women. Once again, John's Gospel supplies "more" detailed accounts "abundant" in meaning.

Each of the segments listed on the next page record times Jesus had an important encounter with a woman. We want to draw conclusions based on all the snapshots rather than staring intently at one picture. Choose a couple of these Scriptures to read. Consider for each what the woman needed, what Jesus gave her, and what the outcome was.

	NEED	WHAT JESUS GAVE HER	THE OUTCOME
John 4:1-39			
John 8:1-11			
John 11:17-44			
John 19:25-27			
John 20:10-18			

REFLECTION

WHICH OF THE WOMEN DO YOU RELATE MOST WITH IN TODAY'S READINGS AND WHY?

Based on these segments, three things about Christ make me fall even more in love with Him.

1. Jesus was not ashamed to be seen with a woman.— At first glance, this point may not seem like a big deal, but how many of us have dated someone who seemed ashamed at times to be seen with us? Beloved, Jesus Christ isn't ashamed to be seen with you. In fact, He wants nothing more! He's also not ashamed to talk to you. I meet so many women who are timid about sharing what they've gleaned in Bible study that week because they "don't have much education" and they're "probably wrong." Listen here, young lady, the One who spoke the worlds into being has chosen you for a Bride! He wants your life to radiate proof that He's been talking to you. He's proud of you!

2. Though very much a man, Jesus understood the needs of a woman.—I despise that ridiculous feminist "theology" that tries to make a woman out of God or at least make Him feminine so we can feel like we have an advocate. Beloved, Christ understands us better than we do ourselves! I'm relieved to know that I am never too needy for Christ … particularly when I'm feeling a tad high maintenance.

In each of the readings you completed, did He leave a single one of those women without acting on behalf of her deep need? No! In every case, He looked beyond the woman's actions and into her heart. He's looking into yours at this very moment and knows what you need even more than you do. Jesus even knows what motivates you to do the things that you do. All that He requires to meet our needs is that we allow Him to draw near to us … talk to us … change us.

3. Without exception, Jesus honored them and gave them dignity.–Do you see a single hint of second-class treatment? In any stretch of the imagination, can you make a woman-hater out of Jesus? Not on your life. A woman-ignorer? No way. How about a womanizer? The mere thought is absurd. Jesus is stunningly personal, intensely intimate, and completely proper. He replaces a woman's shame with dignity. He brings resurrection life to her loss. And, Dear One, He appoints and approves her good works. No, Mary of Bethany wasn't called to preach … but

Christ said her story would be preached throughout the world. Mary Magdalene? She was the very first to spread the good news! The adulterous woman? Surely she got her life together. Maybe even married a fine man and had a family. After all, that's what happened to the prostitute Rahab who appears in the genealogy of Jesus. And Martha? Personally, I think she invented air freshener.

More Relationship

KEY SCRIPTURE

JESUS SAID TO THEM, "MY FATHER IS ALWAYS AT HIS WORK TO THIS VERY DAY, AND I, TOO, AM WORKING." —JOHN 5:17

People are created with a need to know something belongs to them. From the time a person is a toddler, he begins testing what is his by process of elimination. Everything is "mine" until he learns from his parents what doesn't belong to him and what can be taken from him. "No, Sweetie, that's not yours; but here's a blanket. It is yours." Perhaps we could say that maturity is learning how to appropriately recognize and handle what is and isn't ours.

What Is Mine?

I don't know about you, but I need to know that a few things really do belong to me. I might tell you to drop by my house this afternoon; but even after 18 years, that stack of bricks really belongs to the bank. For most of us, this holds true of our cars as well. When we really consider the facts, each of us can call very few things in life "mine." Like the toddler, we also learn often by the process of elimination. I have insisted a few things were mine that God found very creative ways to disprove.

Can you relate? What is something you would like to have called "mine" (yours), but life experiences proved otherwise?

I am convinced that a certain need to possess is so innate in all of us that if we could truly not call anything our own, our souls would deflate with hopelessness. Please hear this: ours is not a God who refuses us possessions. He's simply protective enough of our hearts not to encourage a death-grip on things we cannot keep. He's not holding out on us. He's not dangling carrots in front of our noses then popping us in the mouth when we lunge to bite the bait. Contrary to much public opinion, God is not playing some kind of sick "I-created-you-to-want-but-will-not-let-you-have" game with us. Quite the contrary. The Author of Life will only encourage us to call "mine" what is most excellent. Most exquisite. To those who receive, God gives Himself.

We Can Possess God

Life has plenty of boundaries and "no trespassing" signs. Part of the human condition is that we confront a never-ending influx of "no's." In the midst of so much that we cannot have, God says to His children, "Forsake lesser things and have as much as you want of … Me." Remember, John 3:34 says God gives His Spirit without limit. While God is the owner and possessor of all things, He freely invites us to be as possessive over Him as we desire. He is my God. And your God. He's the only thing we can share lavishly without ever lessening our own supply.

All Things Belong to Christ

When Christ came to this planet, He gave up many of His divine rights in order to accomplish His earthly goals. John 1:2-3 tells us through Him all things were made. Yet Christ didn't walk around saying: "Hey, Bud, do you see that dirt you're walking on? Who do you think made that? In fact, what do you think I made you out of? It's on the bottom of your shoes, Buddy. And that's what you'll be again one of these days if you don't watch your step!"

When we consider that Jesus Christ came to earth as the fullness of the godhead bodily, He actually showed amazing restraint in exercising His divine rights. Matthew 26:53-54 offers one example.

Why did Jesus exercise restraint over His divine rights in this scene?

> **He was with God in the beginning. Through him all things were made. —John 1:2-3**

> **Do you think I cannot call on my Father, and he will at once put at my disposal more than twelve legions of angels? But how then would the Scriptures be fulfilled that say it must happen in this way?—Matthew 26:53-54**

Another reason Christ exercised such restraint was because He had nothing to prove to Himself. John 13:3 says, "Jesus knew that the Father had put all things under his power, and that he had come from God and was returning to God." He knew.

The Right Jesus Claimed

Jesus made a point of fully exercising one right, however; and He constantly angered the Jews when He did so. That "right" was the center of the argument recorded in John 5:16-18. Approximately 110 times out of 248 references to God as Father in the New Testament are found in the Gospel of John. I have become more and more convinced that John's Gospel may have been inspired to be intentionally more relational than the others.

Relationship came to mean everything to the apostle John. From now on, when you think about John, immediately associate him with the one wholly convinced of Jesus' love. In turn, John had much to say about not only reciprocal love but also love for one another. We will see the concept only swell over the remaining weeks of our study.

Christ knew His constant references to God as His Father incited the Jews to riot; yet He was so insistent, He had to be making a point. Through His actions and expressions Christ seemed to say, "I've set aside My crown, My position, My glory, and soon I'll set aside My life for all of you. Hear me well, I will not lay down my Sonship. God is My Father. Deal with it."

The Son of Man had no place to call His own. He had no wife. He had no children. He had no riches, though the diamond and gold mines of the world belonged to Him. He laid claim to nothing. He laid aside everything to come to earth and wrap Himself in human flesh. Taking on our humanity, He also took on our most intrinsic need. In all the loss and sacrifice, He needed something He could call "Mine." "I and the Father are one" (John 10:30). Christ came to earth with nothing but His Father … and He was non-negotiable.

> Jesus said, "Do not hold on to me, for I have not yet returned to the Father. Go instead to my brothers and tell them, 'I am returning to my Father and your Father, to my God and your God.'"—John 20:17

Returning to the Father

The revolutionary message Christ told Mary Magdalene to extend to His disciples (past and present) in John 20:17 can be grasped only in context with Jesus' magnificent obsession with His Father throughout the book. Read this verse.

Record your fresh impressions considering all we've studied today.

Dear Child of God, if you and I were as unrelenting in exercising our rights of sonship (or daughtership), our lives would be transformed. Satan would never be able to dislodge us from God's plan and blessing. You see, Christ had to make the decision to lay aside many rights; but because He retained the most important one of all, His right of Sonship, Satan could not win. Christ led many sons to glory and got to once again pick up every right He laid aside.

Your Right to Sonship

As those who have received Christ's Spirit of Sonship, the same is true for us. Times may arrive when God asks us to lay down the right to be acknowledged in a situation. Or the right to give our opinion or take up for ourselves. The right to withhold fellowship when the other person has earned our distance. The right to be shown as the one who was right in a situation. The right to our dignity in earthly matters.

REFLECTION

HAVE YOU EVER FELT AS THOUGH SATAN WAS ATTACKING YOU? IF SO, DESCRIBE WHAT YOU DID TO THWART HIS PLANS.

But let this truth be engraved on your heart: You will never be required to lay aside your rights of sonship nor must you ever fall to Satan's temptation to weaken your position. As long as you exercise your rights of sonship, constantly reminding yourself (and your enemy) who God is and who you are, Satan will never be able to defeat you or thwart any part of God's plan for your life. Any loss or other right God permits or persuades you to lay aside is temporary. You will ultimately receive a hundredfold in return.

Hold your position, Beloved! Never let anything or anyone talk you out of exercising your rights of sonship! The very reason Satan targets us is because we are the sons (or daughters) of God. He is defeated when we refuse to back off from our positional rights. The last thing he wants to hear from you is, "I am a born-again child of God, and I exercise my right to rebuke you! You, devil, are defeated. You can't take me from my Father nor my Father from me." So, say it!

No matter what you may lose or lay aside, you can call the Father of life "mine"! As His child, you have 24/7 direct access. God will never turn a deaf ear to you nor look the other way when you are treated unjustly. You aren't left to hope He hears you, loves you, or realizes what's going on. Know it, child. Never view your situation in any other context than God as your Father and you as His child.

As we conclude, think carefully about your current challenges. Are there ways you may be trying to hold onto all sorts of rights that are completely secondary, yet not exercising the most important right you have?

Chapter Six

LETTERS TO THE CHURCHES

John wrote to the churches to encourage them and to warn them against following false teachings.

KEY SCRIPTURE

WE PROCLAIM TO YOU WHAT WE HAVE SEEN AND HEARD, SO THAT YOU ALSO MAY HAVE FELLOWSHIP WITH US. AND OUR FELLOWSHIP IS WITH THE FATHER AND WITH HIS SON, JESUS CHRIST.
—1 JOHN 1:3

Christian Fellowship

Years passed. His beard grayed. The calluses on his feet thickened with age. While some scholars believe that John's Gospel and his letters were written within just years of one another, few argue that the epistles slipped from the pen of anything other than an aging man. First John is believed to have been written around A.D. 85-90.

The Passing Years

John had celebrated many Passover meals since the one when he leaned his head against the Savior's strong shoulder. So much had happened since that night. He'd never get the picture of Christ's torn frame out of his mind, but neither would he forget his double take of the resurrected Lord. The fire of the Holy Spirit fell; then the blaze of persecution seared. One by one the other apostles were martyred. People changed and landmarks vanished. Just as Christ prophesied, Herod's temple, one of the wonders of the ancient world, was destroyed in A.D. 70.

For most of us, age means sketchy memories and vague details. Not for John. Read 1 John 1:1-4. According to verse 3, why did the disciples proclaim what they had seen and heard?

With whom is this fellowship?

Fellowship with God

The Greek word for "fellowship" is *koinonia*. Beloved, you and I can be saved to the bone and yet blend in perfectly in our schools and neighborhoods. Goodness knows, carnal and ineffective Christianity is rampant. I can say that without condemnation because I've practiced both. Our fellowship with the very presence of God is the only thing that sets us visibly apart.

> **"I have told you this so that my joy may be in you and that your joy may be complete."**
> **—John 15:11**

I love verse 4. At this point in John's life, he was beginning to sound a lot like his Teacher. (See John 15:11.) Based on our previous discussions of John 15 and John 17, do you grasp that Jesus so thoroughly enjoyed His relationship with His Father and with His followers that He wanted everyone else to enjoy it, too?

Beloved, my koinonia with the Father and Son is light-years from the apostle John's; but I do know what he's talking about. I so thoroughly love and enjoy seeking and finding the living, breathing Son of God that I cannot stand for others to miss it. I want others to fellowship with me as I fellowship with Him!

In Him Is No Darkness

The next verses in 1 John 1 describe some of the reasons why this koinonia is so precious to me. Read 1 John 1:5-10 and fill in the blank below.

God is light; in Him there is no _____ at all (v. 5).

Dear One, I've seen such a dark side of life. I have seen darkness in people of light. I then nearly lost hope in life as I faced the dark side of my own self. We can run from the reminders of the dark side of this world, but we cannot hide … for we'd find them in ourselves. If we stick our heads out of our shells at all, the newspapers and magazines are full of reminders. In the time it takes you to complete this day's study, a father has been murdered, a woman has been raped, and a child has been abused. At times I read specific accounts and feel as if I can hardly bear to stay on this planet another minute. What keeps us hoping and believing amidst this "God-forsaken world"? It is knowing that God has not forsaken this world and that He is light and in Him is NO darkness at all.

70

Sweet One, God has no dark side. Hear that! Absorb it to your marrow! No matter how many theological questions remain unanswered to you, of this you can be sure: God has no dark side at all! You see, that's why He can purify all of us no matter how dark our sides have been. Do you see that His total lack of darkness is also why you can trust Him? He is incapable of having an impure motive where you are concerned.

Staying in His Fellowship

The safety I find in Christ and the pure "blast" He is to me make me desperately want to stay in fellowship with Him. You, too?

First John 1:9 tells us the secret to sharing a life of fellowshiping with Christ and walking in the light. "If we _____ our sins…"

> If we confess our sins, he is faithful and just and will forgive us our sins and purify us from all unrighteousness.—1 John 1:9

The basic Greek word for "confession" is *homologeo,* which is derived from two other words. *Homou* means "at the same place or time, together." *Lego* means "to say."[1] In essence, confession is agreeing with God about our sins. The portion of the definition that holds the primary key to remaining in koinonia is the expediency of "the same place or time." I have confessed and turned from some sins in my life that profoundly interrupted koinonia. Why? Because I waited too long to agree with God about them and turn. I still found forgiveness, but koinonia was broken during the delay. As God began to teach me to walk more victoriously, I learned to often respond to the conviction of the Holy Spirit at the "same place or time" thereby never leaving the circle of fellowship or the path of "light." You see, some of us think fellowship with God can be retained only during our "perfect" moments.

How does 1 John 1:8 in the context of a chapter on true fellowship refute that philosophy?

> If we claim to be without sin, we deceive ourselves and the truth is not in us. —1 John 1:8

Think of koinonia as a circle representing the place of fellowship. We don't just walk in and out of that circle every time a flash of critical thinking bolts through our minds. I don't even think we leave that circle if a sudden greedy, proud, or lustful thought goes through our minds. If we're in koinonia with God, the conviction of the Holy Spirit will come at that place and time and tell us those thoughts or initial reactions aren't suitable for the saints of God. If we respond something like the following, we never depart koinonia. "Yes, Lord, You are absolutely right. That's not how I want to think. I do not desire to entertain those kinds of destructive thoughts. Forgive me and help me to have thoughts that honor You and won't harm me." Confession without delay not only helps keep us in koinonia; it is part of our koinonia!

Accepting Forgiveness

The only thing we accomplish when we leave our sins in the dark is opening a door for the enemy to tempt us to the next level. Ultimately his goal is that we heap sin upon sin. Our joy and protection is right in the circle of koinonia light! Here's one catch: We can respond to conviction and agree with God expediently over our sin and still inadvertently exit the circle of koinonia. How? By refusing to accept and believe God's forgiveness and our fresh purification.

REFLECTION

HOW DO YOU ENSURE THAT YOUR FELLOWSHIP WITH GOD REMAINS STRONG?

You see, agreeing with God over our forgiven state is just as important as agreeing with God over our sin! If Satan can't tempt us to hide our sin and refuse to confess, he'll tempt us not to accept our forgiven and purified state. If we persist in feeling badly, we will think destructively and ultimately act on it. Don't let the devil get away with that! Koinonia is your right in Jesus Christ! Make His joy complete.

KEY SCRIPTURE

HOW GREAT IS THE LOVE THE FATHER HAS LAVISHED ON US, THAT WE SHOULD BE CALLED CHILDREN OF GOD! AND THAT IS WHAT WE ARE! —1 JOHN 3:1

🌴 God's Love for Us 🌴

I can hardly type for wanting to rub my hands together and say, "Hot dog! Let's get to the love!" John chose to believe and fully receive the love of Christ above all other things. What was the result? Like Solomon who asked for wisdom and became the wisest man in history, John prioritized love and became a flooding wellspring of affection. When God esteems our prayers, we get what we ask for and far more.

John's entire focus in his first epistle was relationship. For the remainder of our focus on 1 John, we'll cut straight to the heart and study his favorite subject: love. First, we'll hear John's heartbeat on God's love for us. Next, we'll hear from John concerning God's love through us.

Read the following segments from 1 John and record something you learn about God's love for you.

1 John 3:1-3

1 John 4:13-18

Love Beyond Reason

I originally learned 1 John 3:1 in the King James Version. "Behold, what manner of love the Father hath bestowed upon us!" If we asked God to help us more accurately grasp the true nature of His love for us, our lives would dramatically change! Because John focused on love, God opened his eyes to "behold" it and his soul to perceive it in ways others couldn't have imagined.

Beloved, God's love for you exceeds all reason. I'm not talking about your pastor, your Bible study leaders, or anyone else you greatly admire in the church. I'm talking about you. First John 4:16 says, "And so we know and rely on the love God has for us." We can't define God's love; but we can behold it, experience it, and rely on it. Have you come to experience and rely on the love God has for you? His love for you and me is an absolute reality, but we can be so emotionally unhealthy that we refuse to experience it and absorb it into our hearts and minds.

The Human Heart

Many people are resistant to God because they imagine Him very condemning. In reality, humans are far more condemning and often emotionally dangerous. Our unhealthy hearts not only condemn us. They condemn others. Our hearts sometimes even condemn God as we decide for ourselves that He can't be trusted and that He doesn't really love us unconditionally. Our natural hearts are very deceitful and destructive on their own. We may have a condemning heart without ever facing it.

Picture a house that has been condemned by the city government. See the sign posted on the door: "Condemned Property." Picture how the property looks in your imagination. Is that your heart? Is it in shambles? Are broken pieces of glass scattered all over it? Has it not only been endangered but also become dangerous? As most of us know, hurt people hurt people. My heart used to resemble a condemned property. Oh, I kept a fresh coat of paint over it so no one would know; but I knew the wreck it was on the inside. I even turned the sign over on the other side and wrote: "Fun person who has it all together … as long as you keep your distance and don't look closely."

Unhealthy hearts come in all sorts of shapes and sizes. Some are cold. Others are indiscriminate. Some have thick walls around them. Some have no remaining boundaries at all. Some are forthright and angry. Others are passive and self-disparaging. Some are completely detached. Others are so attached that the object of affection smothers.

We don't have to be raised in severely dysfunctional homes to develop unhealthy hearts. All we have to do is expose ourselves to life. Life can be heartless and mean. Purely and simply, life hurts. We can't check ourselves out of life, however. Instead, God hopes that we'll turn to Him to heal us from the ravages of natural life and make us healthy ambassadors of abundant life in an unhealthy world.

Just between you and God, what is the shape of your heart right now?

Besides God, what are a few things you really do rely on and why?

REFLECTION

HAVE YOU COME TO EXPERIENCE AND RELY ON THE LOVE GOD HAS FOR YOU? EXPLAIN.

Signs of an Ailing Heart

Let me suggest two sure signs of an ailing heart: (1) You're convinced that nothing in life is reliable. Code name: Jaded. (2) You keep trying to convince yourself you can rely on something that has proved unreliable over and over again. Code name: N. Denial.

In case you have a heart like the one I had, please know that God can heal your heart no matter what got it in such a condition. Read 1 John 3:19-20. God is greater than your heart! And He knows everything! Even the thing you secretly believe makes you unlovable … and unloving. Knowing all things, God loves you lavishly. Perfectly. Unfailingly. If He can heal my shattered, self-destructive heart, He can heal anyone's.

Perhaps you've allowed the enemy to hang a "condemned" sign on your heart and you've almost given up on authentic love. Perhaps he's even talked you into becoming a cynic. Beloved, Satan is a liar! He knows if you and I take this thing about God's love seriously, we might become a "John" or a "Paul" in our generations. Oh, let's glorify God, spite the devil, and do it! It's not too late. Take your pulse. If your heart is still beating, it's worth healing! Here's the catch, however: God's method of healing a condemning heart is to love it to death … then create in us a new heart. A healthier heart. A heart filled with faith instead of fear. His perfect love is the only thing that will drive out that fear of ours. (See 1 John 4:18.)

At this season of your life, deep down in your heart, what are a few things you're most afraid of?

No Fear in Love

Fears are fillers. Mind fillers. Heart fillers. Soul fillers. The enemy fuels them because they leave virtually no space for the filling of the Spirit and the welcomed flood of divine love. Second Timothy 1:7 (KJV) tells us that "God hath not given us the spirit of fear; but of power, and of love, and of sound mind."

Based on this verse, why would Satan want to do everything possible to supply us with fillers other than the Holy Spirit?

Satan doesn't want us to know who we could be, nor does he want us to know what we could do. Lives full of God's power, love, and soundness of mind are a terrible threat to the kingdom of hell. After all he's done to me and to so many others, I want to be a threat. Don't you? How do we begin? By allowing God's perfect love to start driving out our destructive fears and condemning natures like an 18-wheeler plowing through a cornfield!

Wholeness begins by deliberately and daily receiving the lavish, unreasonable, unfailing love of God all the way into our marrow. When life is too foggy to "see" the evidences of His love around us, "behold" it in His Word, Dear One! Know it until you feel it.

KEY SCRIPTURE

IF ANYONE SAYS, "I LOVE GOD," YET HATES HIS BROTHER, HE IS A LIAR. FOR ANYONE WHO DOES NOT LOVE HIS BROTHER, WHOM HE HAS SEEN, CANNOT LOVE GOD, WHOM HE HAS NOT SEEN.
—1 JOHN 4:20

God's Love Through Us

No matter how different our personalities, gifts, styles of worship, or denominations, God's chief priority for every single one of us is that we love Him with everything in us. His first priority cannot flow apart from the second: that we love others as ourselves. Read Mark 12:28-31.

Trusting God's Love

One the biggest hang-ups many believers have in loving God and others lavishly is a distrust of the immutable fact of God's love! Everything begins there. How can a person get on with loving God and loving others? He or she can consider all God has said and done to prove His love through His Word and His Son. Then, he or she can confess the sin of unbelief and choose daily to act upon what God has said and done, regardless of the ebb and flow of his or her emotions. How life would change!

Let's take a look at a few things John has to say about loving others in his first letter. Note what each segment teaches about love in the space provided.

1 John 3:16-18

1 John 4:7-8

1 John 4:18-21

1 John 5:3-5

The Difficulty of Loving

Admit it. Loving is a mammoth challenge. Loving God can be challenging, frankly, because He is invisible. Developing what John called an "answering love" requires the active participation of faith and the willingness to learn to "live by the Spirit." (See Gal. 5:16.)

Somehow I don't find loving God quite as challenging as loving a few others I've known. Our most serious challenges are usually not with circumstances. They're with people. My youngest daughter called from college recently on a rampage about someone she "just cannot stand." She is a God-seeking young woman with a fiery passion for His Word, but she agrees with most of us who feel we could serve others more successfully if others weren't so … otherly! I reminded her of a difficult relational challenge she had the year before. Then I "consoled" her with the assurance that she'd have another next year … and the next. Why? Because loving people we find difficult is important to God.

When I began today's lesson I intended to use the phrase "loving difficult people"; but under the direction of the Holy Spirit, I changed the description to "loving people we find difficult." As hard as this suggestion may be on our egos, just because we find someone difficult to love doesn't make him or her a difficult person.

So what's a believer to do with all the challenges to love people we find difficult? Forget faking it. Romans 12:9 already blew our cover on that one. You and I are called to the real thing. God already knew that commanding us to love others sincerely would force the issue of heart change in those who truly desire to obey and please Him.

Draw from God's Agapao

While loving others God places in our paths will never cease to be challenging, the key is learning to draw from the resource of God's own *agapao* rather than our own small and self-ish supply of natural *phileo*, or fondness. Agapao is many things we imagine as love, but two primary elements set it apart. Agapao begins with the will. The beginning of true love is the

REFLECTION

WHO DO YOU FIND DIFFICULT TO LOVE? BEGIN PRAYING FOR THAT PERSON, AND SEE IF YOUR ATTITUDE IMPROVES.

Love must be sincere.
—Romans 12:9

> "I tell you who hear me: Love your enemies, do good to those who hate you." —Luke 6:27

> God has poured out his love into our hearts by the Holy Spirit, whom he has given us.
> —Romans 5:5

> The fruit of the Spirit is love, joy, peace, patience, kindness, goodness, faithfulness, gentleness and self-control.—Galatians 5:22-23

willful decision to agree with God about that person and choose to love. Secondly, when agapao and phileo love are distinguishable, agapao love is based on best interest while phileo love is based on common interests.

Phileo love often originates through preference and taste as in a naturally developed friendship. Agapao tends to be the more "expensive" love because the element of sacrifice is part of its nature. God's directive to love in places like Luke 6:27 involves agapao. It's simply harder and necessitates will at times over emotion.

First John 4:7 tells us love comes from God. It's not from our own determination. Our will is involved in choosing to receive and exercise God's love—not our own.

Romans 5:5 displays the concept beautifully. How does God's love get into our hearts?

What is the first fruit, or trait, of the Spirit in Galatians 5:22?

Based on these two Scriptures, how can we love others more effectively and sincerely?

God knows that challenges like loving someone we find difficult will place the obedient in the position to come to Him constantly for a fresh supply of His love. We have to pour out our own toxic and preferential affections so our hearts can be filled with His affections. As we ask for our cups to overflow with agapao, the liquid, living love of God will not only surge through our own hearts but also splash on anyone nearby. Glory!

KEY SCRIPTURE

THE ELDER, TO THE CHOSEN LADY AND HER CHILDREN, WHOM I LOVE IN THE TRUTH— AND NOT I ONLY, BUT ALSO ALL WHO KNOW THE TRUTH. —2 JOHN 1:1

🐟 Love in the Truth 🐟

I'm having a bad day. A really bad day. This happens every year. I don't plan it. It just happens. I have a bad case of anniversary grief. The silly thing is, the day isn't the anniversary of anything tragic. It was one of the sweetest days of my whole life—the day our son came to live with us. My head was so full of dreams that night. I had never seen a more beautiful little boy. He looked so much like Keith. He played with Keith's plastic fishing worms while I planned his whole future in my head. He would be my man-child. The one I had always wanted.

For reasons known to God, the dreams spun in my head that first night were not to be. Our son of seven years was taken from us. The whole situation has been hard to understand and impossible to explain. God, however, has gone out of His way to clearly state that we are not to interfere. We were on temporary assignment, and He'll let us know if and when He has further need for us. Period.

Every other day of the year I can look at my life through a telescope and sit in utter amazement. God has fulfilled dreams I couldn't have had sense enough to dream. He has done the unimaginable. He delivered me from a life of defeat and deep bitterness. He saved my marriage. Had anyone told me 25 years ago that I'd still be wild about my husband a quarter of a century later and have two young adult daughters who are crazy about Jesus, I might have thought they were dreaming. I also would have not believed anyone who told me that God's scandalous love would allow such a former pit-dweller like me to serve someone like you. Oh, He has been indescribably graceful to me … just like He has to you. On hard days we just need to pull back the lens a little and look at the wider picture. But on these "microscope days" when we determine to slap the most upsetting thing we can think about on a slide and stare at it for hours, we throw a pity party and resent any loved one who refuses to come.

What do you tend to focus on during a microscope day?

REFLECTION

WHAT LIES FROM SATAN HAVE YOU BELIEVED?

The Attack of Lies

Let me warn you. Satan will rarely refuse to attend a good pity party. I appreciate the way Psalm 18:17-18 exposes the opportunism of an enemy. Of God David wrote, "He rescued me from my powerful enemy, from my foes, who were too strong for me. They confronted me in the day of my disaster, but the Lord was my support." Don't think for a moment that Satan won't confront you on the day of your disaster … whatever that may be. Sometimes we give him credit for having a heart and respecting when something should be off limits. After all, fair fighters don't hit a person when she's down.

Satan is not a fair fighter. He confronts us on our worst days and approaches us with his specialty: lies. You can't imagine the lies he tries to tell me on my microscope day. Lies like: "You didn't love the child well enough. You failed him. You failed God. If you had just tried this … or that. If you had waited a little longer." Other times he tries a different approach: "Never take that kind of risk again. Taking someone into your heart like that isn't worth it. You will always get hurt. Love will fail you. Don't let anybody hurt you again."

Just about the time I want to default back to my old coldness, the Spirit of God within me whispers warm breath upon my cooling heart, "My little child, love comes from God … whoever does not love does not know God because God is love."

Truth Sets Us Free

Read the one-chapter epistle of 2 John. Let's stay with our microscope a moment longer. My favorite words in this brief letter are "love in the truth." Does that phrase puzzle you?

Truth sets us free. God, the Great I Am, is the totality of wholeness, completeness, and self-existence. He is both truth and love! While Satan approaches us with hate and lies, we can be "loved in the truth" by God and those His Spirit fills. Our God will tell us only the truth; and one of His chief truths is that loving is always worth doing.

I feel much better. Sometimes I just have to talk it out. I'm ready to put up my microscope and go back to my reading glasses because 2 John also has a few other things to say.

God in Flesh

Scholars admit that 2 John may very well have been written to an actual woman and her children. Many, however, believe that the address was more likely metaphoric to hide the identity of New Testament believers in a time of fierce persecution. If the letter fell into the wrong hands, no one could be singled out. The letter may well have been written to a church.

After calling the chosen lady and her children to walk in love, what warning does John give them?

> Since we have confidence to enter the Most Holy Place by the blood of Jesus, by a new and living way opened for us through the curtain, that is, his body, and since we have a great priest over the house of God, let us draw near to God.
> —Hebrews 10:19-22

No sooner was truth revealed than Satan went on the offensive with lies. Deception is his specialty, and his obvious goal is to get us to believe the lies. Therefore, they can't be blatant or we'd recognize them. Notice nothing is said about these false teachers. Some of the false teachers in John's day did not refute that Jesus was divine. They simply said He wasn't man as well as God. John focused on this exact false teaching in his first letter. Read 1 John 4:1-3. Why is the issue of Christ coming in the flesh so vital? The answer is inferred beautifully in Hebrews 10:19-22. Read these verses carefully.

Exactly how have we gained access to the Most Holy Place, meaning the very presence of God?

The good news of Jesus Christ was running rampant all over the middle-eastern part of the world in John's day and heading north, south, east, and west. Jesus was a hot topic of conversation. Once Satan established that he couldn't squelch spiritual hunger nor stop the talk about Christ, he determined to supply a new story that made best use of both. He suggested through false teachers that Christ indeed came, but not in the flesh. Therefore, the spiritually hungry could still have a belief system involving God but remain, as my relatives would say, as lost as a goose. Why? Because our access to God is through the torn flesh of Jesus Christ. To deny the incarnation is to deny the one and only means of salvation.

I imagine you know someone at school who may be very "spiritual" but doesn't believe in the incarnate death of Christ as the means to salvation. If so, without labeling the belief system, briefly describe it.

Test the Spirits

Do you see what Satan has done? He has tried to feed peoples' need for the spiritual but keep them blind to the truth. Clever and terribly destructive, isn't he? Don't judge them. Pray like mad for them! Pray for the veil to be removed and the torn veil of Jesus' flesh to be made clear!

Pray as well for those who teach such false doctrines. John warned "the chosen lady" not to take any such teacher into her house. In those days, of course, most gatherings of believers met in what we now call house churches. In many countries, they still do.

Recently I spoke in a denominational church I haven't often had the privilege to serve. The pastor stood in the back of the sanctuary and listened to every word I taught. Someone asked me if I was bothered by his presence. I assured them I had nothing but respect for a pastor who watched over his flock so carefully. I was also quite relieved when I passed his test!

In his second letter, John certainly said volumes in so few words. If only I could do the same. One of the things I like best about him is his balance. "Love one another!" And while you're at it, "Test the spirits!" Now, that's a fine teacher.

Body and Soul

John's third letter leaves no doubt that he addressed it to a specific individual. In fact, John drops several names in this one-chapter letter. Read 3 John.

Imagine being named in a letter that turned out to be inspired Scripture for all the world to see! Whether in commendation or criticism, having your name immortalized in Scripture is a heavy thought! When I see a portion of Scripture with brief testimonials similar to the segment we're studying today, I almost shiver.

If just one sentence were written in Scripture about your life at this point in time, what would it be?

KEY SCRIPTURE

DEAR FRIEND, I PRAY THAT YOU MAY ENJOY GOOD HEALTH AND THAT ALL MAY GO WELL WITH YOU, EVEN AS YOUR SOUL IS GETTING ALONG WELL. —3 JOHN 1:2

Loving to Be First

A number of times in my life I would have been devastated over what might have been written in a theoretical one-sentence statement about my life. I love knowing that as long as we're kicking and breathing, we can change the course of our testimonies. God hasn't put a period at the end of our sentences yet, but that tiny little dot doesn't take long to jot.

John obviously had people in his life who were difficult to love. Poor Diotrephes. You'd think with a name that hideous, he wouldn't have wanted to be first. Can you imagine such a one-sentence testimonial? "Beth loved to be first and didn't like to have anything to do with the common folks." Egads! The hair on the back of my neck is standing up!

Notice John didn't say the man was lost. He was obviously a member of the church; and though his actions weren't loving, he could easily have been a Christian. If gossip and divisiveness are unquestionable signs of "lostness," the few folks that go to heaven are liable to have considerable elbow room. Thank goodness we won't have hard feelings and conflict in Glory. Otherwise, I could almost imagine Diotrephes saying to John, "Did you have to go and write it down? Why couldn't you have just gossiped like I did?"

REFLECTION

HOW ARE YOU TAKING
CARE OF YOUR BODY,
THE TEMPLE OF THE
HOLY SPIRIT?

Good Health

Gaius, on the other hand, wasn't only John's dear friend. He was John's dearly loved friend. I hope you didn't miss John's desire for Gaius to be as healthy in body as he was in soul. My Beloved, you and I need to do what we can to watch after our health! Certainly our spiritual health is paramount; but while we're on this earth, the Spirit of God dwelling in each redeemed person is linked explicitly to our physical bodies.

God has taught me serious lessons about the impact my physical body has on both my soul and my spirit. Think about the soul for a moment. If my body is completely exhausted, my soul is deeply affected and over time can absorb the physical weariness and translate it into depression or feelings of hopelessness. If we eat poorly, we can fuel untold anxiety and fear. Stress is linked to heart problems, high blood pressure, and innumerable digestive problems. As long as our souls and spirits are imprisoned in these physical bodies, they are greatly affected by their condition.

You and I live stressful lives. I can't even imagine some of your challenges. I never dreamed I would have the challenges I face today. I am so grateful and humbled by God's present calling on my life to minister to women, but I will not kid you. It is work! Yes, God does most of it all by Himself; but the little He requires from me takes everything I've got!

My dear co-laborer, you and I can't effectively fulfill our callings if we don't watch after our health. Our bodies are temples of the Holy Spirit. At times when I get sick, I know my schedule is out of control again, Satan is on the offensive, or God is checking me out of the loop for a while. All of us deal with illness, but I think God's expectation is for us to do everything reasonable to avoid poor health. Meanwhile, we've got to keep our heads on straight about our motivation. Satan simply wants us in bondage. He loves the bondage of poor health; but he also delights in the yoke of excessive, compulsive fretting over the physical body.

The following verses suggest practices that tremendously impact our physical health. What does each propose?

Psalm 127:2

Matthew 11:28

Mark 6:30-32

Sabbath Moments

Beloved, I am convinced one of our severest needs is pure rest. That includes not only sleep, but refreshment and recreation as well. Recently God spoke to me about capturing what He and I are calling "Sabbath moments." God spoke to my heart one Saturday morning while I was preparing for Sunday School: "My Child, in between more intense rests, I want to teach you to take Sabbath moments."

I once kidnapped my hard-working staff for a few hours to go play a practical joke on another staff member who was running an errand. We hid in the store and had her paged to a department where we "grown Christian women" were hiding in the clothes rounders. We rolled all over the carpet with laughter at the look on her face. After we made complete fools of ourselves, one of the sales ladies walked up to me and said, "Don't I know you from somewhere?" We went to pieces. And then we went back to work … the better for it, I might add.

Sabbath moments! We live in a hard world. You need some Sabbath moments to help you keep your head on straight. Start taking them!

1. Spiros Zodhiates, *The Complete Word Study Dictionary: New Testament* (Chattanooga, TN: AMG Publishers, 1992), 1045-1046.

Chapter Seven

MESSAGES TO THE CHURCHES

Christ spoke to His churches through John.

KEY SCRIPTURE

I, JOHN, YOUR BROTHER AND COMPANION IN THE SUFFERING AND KINGDOM AND PATIENT ENDURANCE THAT ARE OURS IN JESUS, WAS ON THE ISLAND OF PATMOS BECAUSE OF THE WORD OF GOD AND THE TESTIMONY OF JESUS.
—REVELATION 1:9

༽༽༽༽༽ Banished to Patmos ༽༽༽༽༽

We will now join John in exile on the island of Patmos (PAT muhs) in the Mediterranean. Don't bother packing your swimsuit. This 6-mile wide, 10-mile long island is not exactly paradise. In John's day, its rocky, barren terrain attracted the eye of the Romans as the perfect place to banish criminals. Under the rule of the Roman emperor Domitian (A.D. 81-96), Christianity was a criminal offense, and the apostle John was certainly guilty of it.

John's Exile

We don't know the detailed reason for John's confinement on the island. The only absolutes we have are those explained by John himself in Revelation 1:9. Read the verse.

I am curious why John, an undeniable Son of Thunder, was exiled rather than killed under the authority of Roman rule like the other apostles. Tertullian was a historian who lived during the generation closely following that of the apostles (A.D. 150-225). Trained in law and educated in philosophy and history in Rome, Tertullian wrote a work called *The Prescription Against Heretics* that included a stunning claim about the apostle John.

> How happy is its [Rome's] church, on which apostles poured forth all their doctrine along with their blood! where Peter endures a passion like his Lord's! Paul wins his crown in a death like John's [the Baptist]! where the Apostle John was first plunged, unhurt, into boiling oil, and then remitted to his island exile![1]

Very few scholars question the reliability of the early traditions held about Peter's death on a cross to which Tertullian referred. Yes, Peter endured crucifixion like his Lord's; yet feeling unworthy to die in exactly the same manner, Peter requested he be crucified upside down. Likewise, I've never read a commentary that cited reason to question the traditional information that Paul was beheaded like John the Baptist. I certainly don't know if the account regarding John's plunge into boiling oil is reliable; but if you ask me if I think such an event is possible, I could only answer yes!

If Tertullian's account has any accuracy, the Romans may have tried to take John's life and in their foiled efforts, banished him to exile on Patmos. His charge may have been failing to die when told. Though a number of chronological orders are proposed for John's stays outside Jerusalem and Judea, I lean toward the following proposition: John lived and ministered in Ephesus first. At some point he made a trip to Rome, where he fell into persecution, then was banished to Patmos where most scholars believe he remained for about 18 months. I am most convinced by the commentators and early teachers who then assign John back to the city of Ephesus where he spent the short time until his death.

The Revelation of Jesus

With these thoughts in mind, perhaps in pencil rather than permanent marker, let's read our introduction to the mysterious and wonderful Book of Revelation. We will search Revelation for insight into the apostle John himself and for the facts and concepts he seemed to want us to know most. Read Revelation 1:1-10.

The most profound revelation in the Book of Revelation is the revealing of Jesus Christ Himself, not only in visions but in authority. List every single title or description of Jesus Christ in Revelation 1:4–8.

The word *revelation* means "unveiling." Thrown onto a boat transferring criminals, John had no idea what God would unveil to him upon the island of Patmos. Imagine John's frail, aging

frame as he held on tightly while the sea vessel tossed its long way across the Mediterranean. Exile was intended not only for overwork and overexposure to elements but also for crazing isolation. The tactic would be wasted on John, just as it can be wasted on us when Satan tries to force us into isolation.

John's long life may have frustrated him. If forced to remain on earth, exile from ministry and isolation from those he loved was certainly not the way he would choose to spend his senior years. I can't imagine at one point or another in the labors forced upon him that John didn't slip on the jagged, rocky surfaces and rip his thinning skin like paper. He had no bedding for his aching body at the end of a day. I also can't imagine that he thought, *Finally! A little peace and quiet for writing a new book!* He couldn't have expected to meet Jesus on that island like he did. Beloved one, how many testimonies do we need to hear before we accept that sometimes the places and seasons we expect Him least, we find Him most? And oddly, sometimes the places we expect Him most, we find Him least.

John had a critical decision to make while exiled on the unkind island. Would he relax his walk with God at the very least and at most resist? After all, no one from his church or ministry was watching. Would he lie down and die? Goodness knows he was weary. Or would John the Beloved love Christ all the more and seek Him with his whole heart amid the rock and wasteland? His answer rises like a fresh morning tide baptizing jagged shore. "On the Lord's Day I was in the Spirit …" And there He was: the Alpha and Omega. The first and last Word on every life. Every trial. Every exile.

To the Church in Ephesus

Without exception in every book or letter John wrote, he was most adamant that we know Jesus Christ Himself. Refresh your mind with the vision of Christ John received. Read Revelation 1:10-20.

In Revelation 1:19 Christ supplies a basic three-part outline for the entire book. What is it?

1.

2.

3.

I believe the vision of Christ as recorded in verses 12-20 may have constituted "what you have seen." Christ's specific address to each of the seven churches in Revelation 2 and 3 may have constituted "what is now." All seven of the cities were locations where believers in Christ lived and practiced their faith at the time of John's exile. All seven cities were located in Asia Minor, and their order in Scripture suggests a very practical route a messenger might take if he began a journey in Ephesus and traveled on to the other six cities. Many scholars believe that "what will take place later" is found after chapter 4.

The Angels of the Seven Churches

Scholars are divided over the exact interpretation of the "angels" of the seven churches. Many believe the angels are literal, celestial beings assigned to each church, since the basic meaning of the word is "messenger"; however, others think the messenger is a man, perhaps the pastor or overseer at each church. Thankfully, the message is the same no matter who Christ deemed messenger. We will spend much of our focused time in Revelation on the messages to the seven churches. The fact that God included the communication in holy writ tells us the messages have something to say to us. In fact, Christ Himself pointed out their relevance to others as He drew all seven letters to a close with a broad invitation. It is recorded first in Revelation 2:7.

Who does Christ invite to hear?

Now, feel the side of your head. Do you feel an ear? You need only one. "He who has an ear,…" If you have one, Jesus would like you to hear what the Spirit says to the churches. The reason is obvious. You and I are people of His church today; we have much to learn from the successes, failures, victories, and defeats of the early churches. The generations may be far removed, but the basic nature of man and the concepts of Scripture remain consistent.

The Letters to the Churches

Read Revelation 2:1-7. The letters have several repeated components that I want you to identify from the very beginning.

1. Christ identified Himself in a specific way corresponding to some element of John's first vision in Revelation 1:12-18.–In Revelation 2:1, Christ told the church in Ephesus that He held "the seven stars in his right hand" and walked among His churches. This corresponds to John's vision in Revelation 1:12-13,16.

2. Christ commended the church based on intimate acquaintance.–While not every letter contains a commendation, all seven include the phrase "I know your …" I practically shudder every time my eyes settle on the Scripture that tells us Christ "walks among the seven golden lampstands." We already know that the lampstands are the seven churches. The verb tense suggests a continuous action. I believe that as surely as Christ "walked" among the churches and knew them intimately in the first century, He walks among our churches today. Based on His intimate knowledge of the church of Ephesus, He commended the believers' hard work, patience, intolerance of evil, testing of false teachers, and perseverance.

3. Also based on His intimate knowledge, Christ issued a rebuke.–His rebuke to the church in Ephesus (Rev. 2:4) was that they did not love Him as much as they first had.

4. Christ instructed each church to do something specific.–In Revelation 2: 5, Christ instructed the church in Ephesus to repent, to turn from their sins.

5. Last, Christ issued an encouragement to overcome.–Celebrate the fact that no condition is utterly irreversible! In each case, Christ invited the church (made up of individual believers) to overcome.

Don't Lose Your Lampstand

Something they (and we) must be aware of is that time is of the essence! Christ told the Ephesus church in verse 5 that if they did not repent and "do the things" they "did at first," He would come to them and remove their lampstand from its place. The terminology doesn't mean they would lose their place in heaven. We lose our lampstand when we lose a vibrant position of godly influence on earth. In other words, we lose our light in the world.

Beloved, you and I can work hard, persevere through extreme difficulty, not tolerate wicked men, and accurately discern false teachers, yet forsake our first love. If God's absolute priority for all followers of Christ is love for Him first and others second, then the absence of such love is sin. I pound this point so that we can do what we must to get onto the business of loving! God says, "Repent!" I'm not sure we'll be able to welcome the resource of love and His means of shedding it abroad in our hearts until we do. *Repent* means "turn." I believe God told them and is telling us to turn from whatever priority has sabotaged our sacred romance with Christ.

The thought occurs to me how often we forsake our first love—our indescribably glorious sacred romance—because we refuse to forsake our grudges and grievances. How many times has Christ watched His beloved ones "give up" intimacy with Him in order to hang on tightly to unforgiveness? We cannot hang onto our sacred romance with Jesus Christ and our bitterness at the same time. We will release one to hang onto the other. Today, Precious One, release the one that is nothing but bondage. Send it forth! Send it not into oblivion but into the hands of the faithful and sovereign Judge of the earth. Grab the neck of Jesus Christ and hang onto Him with every breath and every ounce of strength you have.

REFLECTION

IS THERE A SIN IN YOUR LIFE THAT YOU NEED TO REPENT OF?

KEY SCRIPTURE

"BE FAITHFUL, EVEN TO THE POINT OF DEATH, AND I WILL GIVE YOU THE CROWN OF LIFE."
—REVELATION 2:10

To the Church in Smyrna

Smyrna (modern Izmir) was an exceptionally beautiful city about 35 miles due north of Ephesus. The people of Smyrna placed a high premium on learning. Science and medicine flourished, contributing to great wealth in the metropolis during the early New Testament era in which John received the revelation. With this landscape picture of Smyrna in mind, read Revelation 2:8-11.

Fill in the characteristic components of Christ's messages to the churches.
Christ's reference to Himself from Revelation 1 (v. 8):

Christ's commendation (v. 9):

Christ's instructions (v. 10):

Christ's encouragement (v. 11):

A Persecuted Church

In the letter to the believers in Smyrna, Christ identified Himself as the "First and the Last." You no doubt noticed the missing rebuke to the church in Smyrna. As Christ walked among this lampstand, He found no fault in her. Impressively, she didn't pass her tests because her exams were easy. To the contrary, no other church is characterized by greater depths of suffering. Christians were despised and terribly mistreated in Smyrna.

"I know … your poverty." Surrounded by wealth, those known to be Christians were persecuted in many ways, not the least of which was economically. Decent jobs were often refused to them and many merchants withheld goods from them.

Christ's comment about the slander of those who say they are Jews and are not, but are a synagogue of Satan, may imply that the Jews in Smyrna identified the Christians to the government and greatly heightened the persecution against them.

Purified by Trials

I recently served on a team with a pastor whose son is dying of a malignant brain tumor. I stood not far from him during praise and worship. This precious father did not deny his immense pain. His tears fell unashamedly, but all the while his worship rose just as unashamed. I believe in the midst of much praise, a fragrance of greater price and exceeding sweetness ascended to the throne from one grieving servant of God.

How are people like my pastor-friend and the believers in Smyrna able to be faithful through such terrible suffering? As resistant as we are to absorb it, one primary reason is inferred in 1 Peter 1:6-9. What do these verses describe?

Those who are faithful in the midst of immense suffering somehow allow their fiery trials to purify them rather than destroy them. We must remember that God grants us grace and mercy according to our need. No, I do not have the strength or character to be faithful under such heart-shattering conditions; but the Holy Spirit will impart a power and grace I've never experienced when my time comes. The challenge is whether or not to accept it.

The believers in Smyrna did not refuse the grace. They inhaled it like air because they were desperate. As much as the church in Smyrna had suffered, Christ warned them of more to come. He did not want them to be afraid. I believe much of the Book of Revelation was written to believers for the same purpose.

Ten Days

We don't know what Christ meant by the time segment of "ten days." Some scholars believe it was literal. Others think it represented 10 years. Still others assume it is a figure of speech for a segment of time known only to God. Whatever the length of trial, Christ called the church of Smyrna to be faithful unto death. His self-identification as the One who died and came to life again reminded them of the absolute assurance of resurrection life. He also promised to reward them with a victor's crown. They would not be touched by "the second death," a term for the final judgment for all unbelievers.

The Martyrdom of Polycarp

Sometimes Jesus defines overcoming not as living well, but as dying well. In other words, dying with faith and spiritual dignity. One of the very saints in Smyrna to which Christ addressed His

REFLECTION

WHEN DIFFICULT TIMES COME, DOES IT HAMPER OR SWEETEN YOUR WORSHIP?

letter left us a profound and wonderful example of an overcoming death. His name was Polycarp. He studied directly under the apostle John's tutelage and was alive at the time Revelation was penned. He became the bishop of the church in Smyrna and served the generation that followed John's heavenly departure. *Foxe's Book of Martyrs* shares the following account of Polycarp's arrest and martyrdom.

> After [ordering a feast for] the guards who apprehended him, he desired an hour in prayer, which being allowed, he prayed with such fervency, that his guards repented that they had been instrumental in taking him. He was, however, carried before the proconsul, condemned.... The proconsul then urged him, saying, "Swear, and I will release thee;—reproach Christ." Polycarp answered, "Eighty and six years have I served Him, and He has done me no wrong. How then can I blaspheme my King who hath saved me?" At the stake to which he was only tied, not nailed as usual, as he assured them he should stand immovable.[2]

Perhaps crucifixion is the only slow death with pain exceeding the fires of a stake. As long as those moments must have been, nothing could have prepared Polycarp for the sight he beheld when death gave way to life and faith gave way to sight. The only Jesus he had ever seen was in the face and heart of John the beloved. That day the old bishop of Smyrna saw the One he loved and served for eighty and six years. Face-to-face. With a victor's crown in His hand.

KEY SCRIPTURE

TO HIM WHO OVERCOMES, I WILL GIVE SOME OF THE HIDDEN MANNA. I WILL ALSO GIVE HIM A WHITE STONE WITH A NEW NAME WRITTEN ON IT, KNOWN ONLY TO HIM WHO RECEIVES IT.—REVELATION 2:17

🎣 To the Church in Pergamum 🎣

About 65 miles above Smyrna, Pergamum was the administrative capital city of Asia and the legal center for the district. Imagine a city with exceeding grandeur. The city boasted not only imposing gymnasiums, theaters, and government facilities, but also a 200,000-volume library that was second only to the library in Alexandria.

Read Revelation 2:12-17 and fill in the pertinent information
Christ's reference to Himself from Revelation 1 (v. 12):

Christ's commendation (v. 13):

Christ's rebuke (vv. 14-15):

Christ's instructions (v. 16):

Christ's encouragement (v. 17):

Satan's Throne

Christ identified Himself to the church of Pergamum as "him who has the sharp, double-edged sword." One primary purpose of a double-edged sword is to divide. As Christ "walked among" the people of this lampstand, He obviously found those who were true to His ways and those who were not. Likewise as He walks among our lampstands today, Christ sees us as individuals who together comprise a church. The faithfulness or rebelliousness of any given individual never gets swept up or "grayed" in the corporate whole. How I wished at times it did!

We can only imagine what kind of warfare they experienced. Christ referred to the city as the place "where Satan has his throne." Since Satan is not omnipresent (present in all places at all times), Christ's claim is hair-raising. We can't be certain what He meant, but historical evidence from the first century tells us Pergamum was the uncontested center of pagan worship in Asia Minor. Keep in mind that Satan's primary goal is to keep people blinded to truth while providing something that momentarily seems to pacify their spiritual hunger. Pergamum delivered. Christ spoke about the church in Pergamum remaining true to His name. Inhabitants had plenty of names to choose from. Within its walls were temples to Dionysus, Athena, Asclepius, and Demeter, three temples to the emperor cult, and a huge altar to Zeus.

When given the opportunity, Satan gladly supplies a counterfeit "savior" providing a dandy benefit package. Any world religion or brand of humanism will do. Since man was created to seek God's benefits, Satan works most effectively if he is able to offer alternatives. For instance, he's sly to suggest other ways for people to unload their guilt. One workable way is to convince them they haven't sinned. He has all sorts of means of providing counterfeit "redemption." Not long ago I received a letter from a loved one with whom I had shared my testimony about the transforming power of God's Word. He, a practicing Buddhist, wrote me his own testimony about how life had improved since he changed his "karma." My heart broke over the inevitable disillusionment of self-worship. At some point surely a self-worshiper looks in the mirror and says, "If I am as good as God gets, life stinks."

Faithful to Death

Though surrounded by counterfeits, Christ's commendation tells us many believers in Pergamum remained true and did not renounce their faith even when Antipas was put to death. Romans 8:31 tells us, "If God is for us, who can be against us?" The day Antipas died, God was for him. Like Polycarp, Antipas stood against all; and he overcame. You and I are going to learn something vital from our study of Revelation: death doesn't always mean defeat.

The Teachings of Balaam

Not every member of the church in Pergamum was a faithful witness like Antipas. Christ rebuked an undesignated number for holding to the teachings of Balaam and the Nicolaitans. We can't identify the "teaching of the Nicolaitans," but they are closely associated with the "teachings of Balaam." The account of Balaam and Balak is found in Numbers 22-24. In a nutshell, Balak, the king of Moab, greatly feared the Israelites as they settled in the Promised Land. He hired Balaam the soothsayer to curse Israel, but he blessed them instead. Balaam did, however, instruct Balak how to defeat the Israelites. He told Balak to seduce them into idolatry through the harlotry of the Moabite women. Based on all I've read, I believe the basic concept of Balaam's teachings is this: if you can't curse them, try to seduce them!

The whole idea makes my blood boil. You see, Satan is waging war on our generation with Balaam's weapon. (See 1 Tim. 4:1!) Satan can't curse us because we are "blessed" (Eph. 1:3) children of God, covered by the blood of the Lamb. If the devil can't curse us, then how can he defeat us? He can try to seduce us! How does seduction differ from temptation? All seduction

is temptation, but not all temptation is seduction. Many temptations are obvious. The aim of seduction is to catch the prey off guard. That's why Satan's best henchmen (or women) are often insiders rather than outsiders. Some in the church of Pergamum were enticed into sin by others among them. Whether or not the seducers were truly saved is unclear. Either way, Christ expected the church to jump into action.

If the seducers were true believers, they needed to be confronted properly and restored when repentant. Some may wonder how believers could be used by Satan to seduce. Beloved, seduced people seduce people. If the devil's scheme is not exposed and the chain is not broken, it perpetuates. Without a doubt, some of Satan's most effective seducers can be within the church. We must develop discernment and guard our hearts jealously without becoming fearful and suspicious. Authentic godliness, rather than religiousness, is our best defense against seduction.

Christ's tenderness and encouragement in Revelation 2:17 must have spared their hearts. What two things did Christ promise to those who overcame?

Christ's Promises

The hidden manna contrasts beautifully with the food sacrificed to idols. Jesus Christ was the Bread of life sacrificed on the altar before the one true God. Now His Spirit falls like manna from heaven to all who hunger.

The most probable meaning of the white stone is remarkable. In an ancient courtroom, jurors voting to condemn the accused would cast their vote by tossing a black stone or pebble. In contrast, jurors voting to acquit the condemned would cast their vote by tossing a white stone or pebble. Scripture actually records this ancient practice, but our English translations don't portray it. Read Acts 26:10. In this verse, Paul testified that he formerly deposited, or cast, his pebble to vote against the saints.

On the authority of the chief priests I put many of the saints in prison, and when they were put to death, I cast my vote against them.—Acts 26:10

The terminology Christ used was perfectly fitting for Pergamum. Do you remember one of the first facts we learned about the city? It was the legal center in the district. How I praise God that the Judge of all the earth pitches a white stone to acquit us. Not because we're innocent. Because Someone already served our sentence. And the new name on the stone? Yes, it could be Christ's; but I also think we each have an overcoming name not unlike Abram/Abraham, Simon/Peter, and Saul/Paul.

To the Church in Thyatira

Forty-five miles east of Pergamum is the city of Thyatira. It can't be explored because the modern city of Akhisar in Turkey stands atop its ancient ruins. Thyatira was not known for her beauty. She was known for her commerce.

Read Revelation 2:18-29 and fill in the pertinent information.
Christ's reference to Himself from Revelation 1 (v. 18):

Christ's commendation (v. 19):

Christ's rebuke (v. 20):

Christ's instructions (v. 25):

Christ's encouragement (vv. 26-28):

KEY SCRIPTURE

NEVERTHELESS, I HAVE THIS AGAINST YOU: YOU TOLERATE THAT WOMAN JEZEBEL, WHO CALLS HERSELF A PROPHETESS.
—REVELATION 2:20

Thyatira found her significance in two identities. The city originally was an important military headquarters. Her military legacy continued under Roman rule, but she evolved into one of the most thriving commercial centers in all Asia. Her city walls bulged with wool and linen workers, dyers, leather workers, potters, tanners, bakers, slave dealers, and bronzesmiths. Many scholars believe Christ described Himself with blazing fire and burnished bronze because inhabitants of Thyatira took such pride in their metal works.

Jezebel

Scripture associates Thyatira with two different women: Lydia and Jezebel. Some scholars believe Jezebel was a real woman who played havoc in the church at Thyatira. I am strongly inclined to agree, but I am also thoroughly convinced she is representative of a kind of woman none of us want to be.

Reread Revelation 2:20-21. Discern everything you can about Jezebel from Thyatira based on this passage and record it here.

Jezebel could have been the woman's actual name, but Christ was far more likely drawing the parallel between the woman in Thyatira and the brazen wife of King Ahab. (See 1 Kings 16–21.) The original Jezebel was raised in Sidon, a commercial city not unlike Thyatira. She married Ahab, a king of Israel, and moved to Jezreel. The city served the one true God, but she determined to turn it into a center of Baal worship. The wicked queen soon became the power behind the throne. Obedient to her wishes, Ahab erected a sanctuary for Baal and supported hundreds of pagan prophets. She massacred the prophets of the Lord when they opposed her.

Fast forward to the New Testament and a woman who bears her predecessor's name. The ancient city of the Bible's Thyatira tells the story of women and power. In 20th century terms, Thyatira was "liberated." Women could be quite successful, which was (and is) admirable. Powerful trade guilds ran the city like the mob runs some cities today. Clubs and societies were

not only social but also political. They were also strangely "religious" because they entrenched their members in all sorts of idolatrous practices. Not only did unethical deals and practices prevail, sexual immorality was rampant. Somehow, extramarital sexual expression got twisted up in their concept of "liberation."

The Abuses of Jezebel

The Revelation 2 Jezebel was a very powerful woman in Thyatira. She was up to her elbows in secret guilds and society climbs and did everything she could to infiltrate the church with them. Lydia was also a powerful woman in Thyatira. (See Acts 16:13-15.) Together they provide a lesson on abuse vs. wise use of authority. You and I live in a culture where women can be very successful and hold many authoritative positions. Many women have strong gifts that float to the top in various professions. That's wonderful … as long as they know what to do with position. When God gifts women professionally, we want to be Lydias. The following characteristics describing Jezebel will help shed light on any shred of her type living in us.

1. Jezebel assumed places of authority God did not assign her.—Revelation 2:20 tells us that Jezebel called herself a messenger of God. The New Testament undeniably records that women were given the gift of prophecy. (See Luke 2:36-38; Acts 2:17-18; Acts 21:8-9.) But Jezebel had no such God-given gift. She wasn't called. She was controlling! She wasn't wisely authoritative. She was bossy! Oh, that none of us would confuse the two! Look again at Revelation 2:21-23! Please don't miss that Jezebel's most serious infraction was not her sin but her unwillingness to repent!

Lydia stands in stark contrast to Jezebel as a woman of success. She was a worshiper of God—not herself or position. She opened her heart to Paul's message rather than pulling rank on him. Both professionally and spiritually, the tone of Scripture suggests she was a servant-leader.

2. Jezebel abused her feminine gift of influence.—Verse 20 tells us that she misled God's servants. I am convinced women have a unique God-given gift of influence. Many accounts in Scripture attest the power of a woman's influence. Eve and Sarai represent some biblical blights; but, thankfully, we can find more scriptural examples of positive womanly influence than negative. Lydia is certainly one of them.

Search Acts 16:15 carefully, noting Lydia's powerful influence. Describe how she used it.

> When she [Lydia] and the members of her household were baptized, she invited us to her home.
> —Acts 16:15

3. Jezebel misused her sexuality (Rev. 2:20).—I'm not sure our culture has taught us to use anything more powerfully than sexuality. Don't think for a moment that seducing someone into having sex is the only way a woman can use her sexuality to manipulate. A woman can be completely clothed and in broad, public daylight and still misuse her sexuality.

Be bold enough to write an example expressing how we can misuse our sexuality.

Sexuality was given by God as a gift. Not a tool. God created women complete with gifts, contributions, and influences. But women need to be women well.

❧ To the Church in Sardis ❧

T he winds of Thyatira at our backs, let's now set our sights on Sardis, about 30 miles southeast. As we travel these miles together, I wonder if you are as sobered as I am by Christ's meticulous attention to all who gather in His Name. We, the people of His churches, carry the reputation of Christ in our cities like those holding banners in a town parade. What does each of our banners say about Him? Christ isn't looking for perfect churches because He knows they are comprised of imperfect people. He is looking for churches that glorify God and lift up Christ by correctly estimating their worth through worshiping, teaching Truth, and living love.

Read Revelation 3:1-6 and fill in the pertinent information.
Christ's reference to Himself from Revelation 1 (v. 1):

Christ's rebuke (v. 1):

Christ's instructions (v. 2):

Christ's encouragement (v. 4):

A Dead Church

If we studied the 7 churches of Asia Minor and 700 more in our cities today, we would quickly discover that the personalities and morals of any given city permeate its churches unless deliberately overcome. For instance, churches in wealthy areas full of upper-crust attitudes will have to overcome misguided superiority to keep from portraying the same things. Why? Because the people that comprise churches are also products of their societies. Likewise churches in cities of deeply ingrained prejudice will carry the same banner unless they deliberately risk being different. A church can be refreshingly dissimilar to its surrounding society only through the deliberate renewing of minds.

We might accurately say that the surrounding city of the church of Sardis was the near "death" of her. You no doubt noted Christ had little to say in favor of this ancient church. Sardis was best known for its "cemetery of the thousand hills" about seven miles from town. A city preoccupied with death, Sardis looked upon a distant skyline of countless burial mounds.

The church in Sardis could not miss the parallel Christ drew concerning their renowned cemetery when He confronted their deadness. He also said, "You have a reputation of being alive." Dead churches. I believe they are one of the most confounding mysteries to the hosts of heaven. The ministering spirits that invisibly flood the atmosphere must look upon the church then back upon the radiance of Jesus Christ and wonder how anything that carries His name can be dead. Above all things, Christ is life! Lifeless churches are made up of lifeless Christians. Thankfully, Christ still raises the dead, but His serious warning was to wake up and respond without delay! Like an athlete who lets his muscles atrophy before the end of his season, the church needed spiritual rehab—beginning by strengthening the little that remained.

KEY SCRIPTURE

WAKE UP! STRENGTHEN WHAT REMAINS AND IS ABOUT TO DIE, FOR I HAVE NOT FOUND YOUR DEEDS COMPLETE IN THE SIGHT OF MY GOD.
—REVELATION 3:2

REFLECTION

IF THE CHURCH YOU ATTEND AND SERVE CARRIED A BANNER REPRESENTING CHRIST, WHAT POSITIVE STATEMENT WOULD IT MAKE?

Since the children have flesh and blood, he too shared in their humanity so that by his death he might destroy him who holds the power of death—that is, the devil—and free those who all their lives were held in slavery by their fear of death.

—Hebrews 2:14

Contributions to Deadness

What invaded the church of Sardis with such deadness? The history of this ancient city suggests three contributors.

1. The people of Sardis were fixated on death rather than life.—Some might ask, "Why would any of us be more fixated on death than life?" We don't have to idolize burial mounds like the Sardians to focus on death more than life. Worship in its simplest essence is attentiveness. One way we can focus on death more than life is to possess a life-inhibiting fear of it. I have known people who were so scared of death they could hardly live life.

What does Hebrews 2:14 have to say about the subject?

REFLECTION

BY ANY CHANCE, DEAR ONE, HAVE YOU OR SOMEONE YOU LOVE INTERPRETED REJECTION AS A DEATHBLOW? IF SO, EXPLAIN.

2. The people of Sardis not only fixated on death but also relied on their past achievements.—The city was like a leading lady in a Greek tragedy who waltzed around town in riches turned to rags thinking everyone still saw her as she was 30 years ago. In essence, Christ wrote the church of Sardis to hand this self-deceived woman a mirror, just like He's handed one to me a time or 10. Christ does not hand someone a mirror to destroy her, however. He hands her the mirror to wake her up!

3. The people of Sardis likely interpreted rejection as a deathblow.—Sardis lost its bid to build a temple to Caesar in A.D. 26. I'd like to hypothesize that the people of Sardis knew they needed a fresh shot of life and vitality when they bid for the new temple. When they were rejected in favor of a rival city, I wonder if they took on an attitude all too common after rejection: *Why should we even try? Who cares anymore?* Unless good reason exists to respond otherwise, rejection can cause people to lose heart faster than almost anything.

Dead Sardis Could Live Again

Perhaps the following commentary sums up the deadness of Sardis at the time of John's vision better than any: "Sardis was a city of peace, not the peace won through battle, but 'the peace of a man whose dreams are dead and whose mind is asleep, the peace of lethargy and evasion.'"[3] This is a stunning statement, not because it speaks so perfectly to an ancient city's decay, but because it speaks to many of us today.

Christ's identity to the church in Sardis is also the key to their resurgence. Christ is the one who holds the "seven spirits of God" or the seven-fold perfect Holy Spirit. Like the day of Pentecost, life infiltrates our churches when God pours out His lavish Holy Spirit upon them. Spirit-flooded churches are built one way: through Spirit-flooded people.

≫≫⊛ To the Church of Philadelphia ≫≫⊛

We have only about 28 miles to travel southeast of Sardis to find Philadelphia, a high plateau city. The city was built in a dangerous volcanic area. Bar an eruption, our visit should be refreshing.

Read Revelation 3:7-13 and fill in the pertinent information.
Christ's reference to Himself from Revelation 1 (v. 7):

Christ's commendation (v. 8):

Christ's rebuke (v. 9):

Christ's instructions (v. 11):

Christ's encouragement (v. 12):

The Church of Little Strength

King Attalus II (159-138 B.C.) established Philadelphia. The city was named "Philadelphus," meaning "brother lover," in honor of his love for his brother. Scholars almost unanimously agree that "I know that you have little strength" was not referring to spiritual strength. Virtually all Bible commentators I studied believe Christ's reference to the "little strength" of Philadelphia's church referred to their small size and small visible impact. Lower, less influential people comprised the church of Philadelphia; yet they endured patiently (v. 10).

Nothing is more destructive than feelings of uselessness and worthlessness. That's precisely why the enemy seeks every avenue to fuel them and every available puppet to perpetuate them. Beloved, each of us has a God-given need to matter. You are not self-centered or vain because you have it. You are human. What you and I do with the need can become extremely vain and self-centered, but the need itself is sacred.

Who Really Matters?

The Father desires for each of our lives to bring forth much fruit. I desperately want each one of you to flourish in the ministries God has for you, and I think the church of Philadelphia offers us a few pointers in the process.

1. Christ alone is judge of what matters.—The small, seemingly insignificant band of believers in Philadelphia may have been blind to the fruit of their own efforts, but Christ found them beyond rebuke. I think the key word in His commendation is the description He used for how they endured: patiently. So often we are tempted to give up before the harvest comes. God promised in Genesis 8:22 that "as long as the earth endures, seedtime and harvest, cold and heat, summer and winter, day and night will never cease." Though they are far less predictable, we experience seasons spiritually as well as climatically. The church in Philadelphia had been in the seedtime season without a large harvest for a long time; yet they continued to endure patiently. Notice what Christ commended the church in Philadelphia for after acknowledging their "little strength" in Revelation 3:8. Unashamed of Christ's name against a bitter majority,

KEY SCRIPTURE

I KNOW YOUR DEEDS. SEE, I HAVE PLACED BEFORE YOU AN OPEN DOOR THAT NO ONE CAN SHUT. I KNOW THAT YOU HAVE LITTLE STRENGTH, YET YOU HAVE KEPT MY WORD AND HAVE NOT DENIED MY NAME. —REVELATION 3:8

REFLECTION

WHY IS THE NEED TO MATTER SACRED? GOD FORMED HIS PRIZED CREATION TO SEEK LIVES OF PURPOSE; AND FOR THOSE WHO WOULD FOLLOW HIS LEAD, WE FIND PURPOSE ULTIMATELY IN HIM ALONE.

they kept Christ's Word, thereby faithfully planting seeds. They did not give up though the harvest seemed dreadfully distant.

A landowner doesn't judge a harvest by the quantity of fruit alone. Diseased fruit means nothing but loss to him. He looks for quality. I can remember pouring my heart into preparing several discipleship courses when only two or three people showed up. I sensed God ask me, "What are you going to do now? Cancel the class? Or give them no less than you would give 25?" I am certain those were not only precious opportunities. They were tests.

2. *Christ is the door opener.*—Notice what Revelation 3:8 tells us about doors: Christ opens … and shuts. One reason for so much frustration in ministry is our determination to open our own doors. In Jesus' name, of course. Some of our fists are bloody from beating down doors that we believe were supposed to open for ministry. When our blood, sweat, and tears produce little or nothing, we are often offended by God who I believe sits upon His throne and says, "Did I tell you that was the right door? If it were, would I not have opened it for you?" I often think of the gate of Peter's prison automatically opening for his escape because God appointed it. (See Acts 12.)

Because the church of Philadelphia endured patiently, Christ placed before them an open door that no one could shut. Many scholars believe that "open door" was for missions directed further due east to other parts of Asia. Hence, some commentators call the church of Philadelphia the "missionary church." Dear One, each of us is called to missions. As we seek to "keep" Christ's Word and stay unashamed of His Name (Rev. 3:8), He will open doors of opportunity for us in His own time. If we faithfully sow seed, the harvest will one day come.

Christ's promise to the overcomers was that they would (1) be kept from the hour of trial that is going to come upon the whole world and (2) stand like pillars in a Kingdom that can never be shaken. Why? Because they mattered and, opposed to popular opinion, chose to believe it. So do you, Dear One. Let no one take your crown by convincing you otherwise.

🌴 To the Church of Laodicea 🌴

Our next and final stop in our discovery of the seven churches addressed in Revelation is Laodicea. We'll find the city 45 miles southeast of Philadelphia and about 100 miles east of our first stop in Ephesus. As we walk through the gates of our last destination in this segment of Revelation, we will have indeed come virtually full circle.

Read Revelation 3:14-22 and fill in the pertinent information.
Christ's reference to Himself from Revelation 1 (v. 14):

Christ's rebuke (v.16):

Christ's instructions (vv. 18-19):

Christ's encouragement (v. 21):

"YOU SAY, 'I AM RICH; I HAVE ACQUIRED WEALTH AND DO NOT NEED A THING.' BUT YOU DO NOT REALIZE THAT YOU ARE WRETCHED, PITIFUL, POOR, BLIND AND NAKED."
—REVELATION 3:17

So many word plays and inferences are in this segment of Scripture that I am frantically asking God to help me choose what to teach and what to leave behind. Many adjectives could apply, but let's consider the following three.

1. The church of Laodicea was indifferent.—Christ—who never desires for anyone to perish— would not prefer someone to be cold toward Him rather than lukewarm. I believe Christ meant, "For crying out loud, be of one use or the other!" We have much to learn about this distinct city that will shed light on Christ's rebuke and exhortation.

The last thing I want to tout is a works-centered faith, but we have been called to faith-centered works. If Christ has left His church in this dark, hurting world for anything, He left us to be useful! Churches are meant to be active forces in their communities, and not just where they have vested interests. Churches have doors not only for the world to come in but also for the church to go out.

In our previous lesson we talked about each person's innate need to matter. In its simplest form, all "mattering" requires is discovering how our gifts and contributions can be useful. If where we matter highly matters to us, we inadvertently slipped from innate need to ego feed. Anyone with the ability to breathe can be useful. In the spirit of Christ's rebuke to Laodicea, anyone can offer a cold glass of water to the thirsty or a hot cup of tea to the hurting. Christ instructs the church, His Bride, "Be of use to my world!" At times therapeutic. At other times refreshing. Each of us can be hot and cold.

2. The church of Laodicea was independent.—The Laodiceans did what many people in our culture do today. They filled their need to matter with possessions and then gauged their usefulness by their wealth. Praise God, neither then nor now can wealth state worth. Laodicea, however, was the capital of financial wizardry in Asia Minor when Christ drafted His letter throughJohn.

How did the church describe herself? (See v. 17.)

Mind you, Christ's letter isn't addressed to the city of Laodicea. It is addressed to the church of Laodicea. How does that hit you? I can almost imagine the preacher glancing at the order of service during worship and saying, "Skip the offertory! After all, we're rich! We do not need a thing!" We'd die of shock at our church. I can't remember a time when we've had more money than needs. The needs out there are endless.

In A.D. 26 the city placed a bid to the Roman Senate to build a temple to the Emperor Tiberius. They were denied on the basis of inadequate resources. Their wealth so vastly increased over the next several decades that by A.D. 60 after the devastation of an earthquake, they didn't accept aid from Nero. They had plentiful resources to rebuild themselves. (Do you hear the hints of independence?)

New money. The Laodiceans had it. Certainly not all those with sudden wealth invest it in their ego accounts and disconnect their servers from the "unfortunate." Furthermore, not all those with "old money" are charitable. The Laodiceans were lying in the lap of luxury and they did

REFLECTION

IN WHAT AREAS OF YOUR LIFE HAVE YOU DECIDED YOU DON'T NEED A THING?

not have a care in the world. Little did they know Christ was walking among their lampstand. Beloved, wealth by itself is not the issue. We serve a God of infinite wealth who can distribute the riches of the world any way He sees fit. Few things can be more "useful" in our troubled world than resources in the hands of wise people. The problem is the undependability and deceitfulness of wealth. The Laodicean Church somehow didn't grasp the principle in Luke 12:48. "For unto whomsoever much is given, of him shall be much required." (KJV)

3. *The church of Laodicea was self-deceived.*–Their worth was so ingrained in their wealth that they honestly saw themselves as utterly independent. We "do not need a thing." Famous last words. Beloved, I'm not sure any of us get away with "not needing a thing" for long. Certainly the kinds and intensities of our needs differ from season to season, but I don't expect God to risk our growing an independent spirit through sustained seasons of sufficiency. Of course, I don't know this for a fact because I can't remember having one. The older I get and the more my eyes open to the facts of life and ministry, the more my list of needs exceeds my list of wants. For instance, I need to have an active, effervescent, daily relationship with Jesus Christ, or I'm sunk. I need my husband's blessing. I need my coworkers. I need my church family. I need a friend I can trust. These are just a few necessities of life to me right now.

Christ's Remedy

How grateful I am that Christ had a remedy for the Laodiceans! Their self-deceived indifference had not deemed them castaways. Christ wrote the Laodiceans a three-part prescription.

- **His first prescription was gold refined in fire.**–Read 1 Peter 1:6-7 for a hint as to what He meant by this.
- **His second prescription was "white clothes to wear."**–The black wool fabric for which Laodicea was famous was the fashion rage all over that part of the world. He suggested they trade their fashions for purity. Ouch.
- **His final prescription was salve to put on their eyes.** Laodicea not only was a marketing center and financial capital, but also housed a well-known medical center. Ever the marketers, they were best known for "Phrygian powder" that was used to make salve for eye conditions. All the while, the Laodiceans were blind as bats and poor as beggars. I've been both.

One thing I've learned about God is that He is most assuredly faithful. In every way. He is faithful to forgive, redeem, bless, provide. And He is also faithful to chastise when His child won't readily turn from sin. Yes, the Laodiceans had a prescription; but Christ had no intention of letting them wait a month of Sundays to get it filled without consequences.

Christ has invested everything on earth in His church. He willingly fills her, frees her, purifies her, and restores her; but He never takes His eyes off of her. Lives are at stake. Church matters. Bride, make yourself ready.

> Now for a little while you may have had to suffer grief in all kinds of trials. These have come so that your faith—of greater worth than gold, which perishes even though refined by fire—may be proved genuine and may result in praise, glory and honor when Jesus Christ is revealed.
>
> —1 Peter 1:6–7

1. Tertullian, *The Prescription Against Heretics*, 36 ANF 3:260.
2. William Byron Forbush, ed., *Foxe's Book of Martyrs* <http://www.reformed.org/books/fox/DOCS/fox102.html> (5 September 2002).
3. Frank E. Gaebelein, et al., eds., *The Expositor's Commentary* 12 vols. (Grand Rapids, Mich.: Zondervan, 1981), 12:448, quoting William Barclay, *Letters to the Seven Churches* (New York: Abingdon, 1957), 72.

Chapter Eight
THE BLESSED BENEDICTION

God revealed to John the victory that will be ours in the end times.

KEY SCRIPTURE

DAY AND NIGHT THEY NEVER STOP SAYING: "HOLY, HOLY, HOLY IS THE LORD GOD ALMIGHTY, WHO WAS, AND IS, AND IS TO COME."
—REVELATION 4:8

⋙ The Throne Room ⋙

Today you and I are going to approach the very throne of God through the vision extended to the apostle John in the fourth chapter of Revelation. If we had any idea who and what we approach when we go to the throne of grace (Heb. 4:16) through prayer and communion with God, our lives would be altered dramatically. I am convinced we not only would fall on our faces far more often but also would pray with far more substance and certainty.

John's Picture of the Throne Room

As you prepare to read Revelation's description of the throne room of God, please keep in mind that John related the completely unfamiliar through the familiar. Imagine escorting someone who had never ventured further than the most primitive part of the Amazon to tour state-of-the-art technology at NASA. When he returned to his fellow tribesmen, how would he describe jets or rockets to them? He'd probably have to begin his illustration using birds as an example and try to stretch their imagination from there. Likewise, throughout much of Revelation John employed known concepts to express images beyond our understanding.

As you read all of Revelation 4, draw a diagram in the margin illustrating each description. Stick figures are fine, no matter how elementary.

Christ's revelation to the apostle John shifts dramatically in the unfolding of chapter 4. In chapters 2 and 3, the spotlight of the Spirit turned to earth to cut through religious appearances, revealing the best and the worst about the seven churches in Asia Minor. In Revelation 4, the spotlight swung back to the origin of all illumination as Christ summoned John heavenward in Spirit to behold the Divine. Heaven was awhirl with activity, yet all attention was stolen by a throne in heaven with someone sitting on it. John describes the splendor of the throne by referring to brilliant gems. When the scales of humanity peel away from our eyes and we behold heaven, I believe we will see colors as never before. Perhaps only the crystal sea will be "clear."

The throne of God is beyond anything we can imagine; yet how does Hebrews 4:14-16 tell us we can approach it and why?

Finding Grace at the Throne

First John 1:8 tells us no one is without sin; however, because Christ became our atoning sacrifice, we need never fear approaching God with our confessions. In the imagery of the throne room, I like to imagine God the Father catching those confessions in the palm of His mighty hand and casting them into the sea. No matter how many confessions are made, this "sea" is never muddied by our sins. Rather, as God casts them into the sea I like to imagine our sins instantly bleached into utter non-existence, swallowed in the depths of crystal clear waters.

Beloved, are you a deep-sea fisherman? In other words, are you tempted by guilt, condemnation, and unbelief to trudge up old sins and agonize over them? Satan constantly volunteers to be our fishing guide, providing a handy lure to cause us to doubt God's forgiveness. I certainly have done some deep-sea fishing in my lifetime. What a waste of time and energy! If we're fishing in the right sea, our line will always come up bare. Anything we "think" we're seeing on the end of that line is a vain imagination.

He Who Sits on the Throne

The throne is never depicted without someone sitting upon it! God never vacates His throne. He is never off duty. His sovereignty is never usurped. He is unceasingly praised. The three-fold acclamation of God's holiness significantly occurs only in the visions of the throne room. Perhaps like me you often look for any distinctions regarding the holy Trinity. Let's discuss what part of the Godhead may be depicted on the throne in these three revelations.

Before we immediately assume God the Father is the occupant, read Revelation 5:6. Where is the Lamb (Christ) depicted as "standing"?

I don't believe the revelator meant us to picture Christ standing up on a chair. Our familiarity with a throne is entirely related to a piece of furniture. Though God is most assuredly sitting in an actual seat of authority (Isa. 6:1), the word *throne* seems to encompass the center from which He presides with all authority. I am intrigued that Ezekiel's vision describes "a figure like that of a man" upon the throne (Ezek. 1:26). According to John 12:41, Isaiah saw Jesus' glory when he beheld the vision in Isaiah 6. Ordinarily the man-like descriptions in the Godhead are attributed by most scholars to Christ. According to Revelation 5, both the Father and the Son inhabit the throne room.

The World from Heaven's Perspective

Beloved, the fixed point in John's vision is the same immutable point in the entire universe. The center of all existence is God upon His throne. John had the hair-raising, perspective-changing opportunity to do something all of us secretly wish we could do. For a little while recorded in Revelation 4 and onward, he got to see life from heaven's perspective. In his description, he implied something tremendously profound: everything else in existence is most accurately described only in its relationship to the throne of God.

God looked upon His prize creation and liked us very much. Look carefully at Revelation 4:11 where much is implied in the original language about God creating us by His will. God's *will* is "an expression or inclination of pleasure; a want or desire which pleases and creates joy."[1] In other words, He created us because it pleased Him. Our attitudes and actions don't always please Him; but creating us, loving us, and redeeming us gives Him great joy.

We often see ourselves as the center of the universe and tend to describe all other components in reference to us rather than God. The human psyche almost invariably processes incoming information in relationship to its own ego. For example, if the news forecasts an economic slump, the natural hearer automatically processes what it could mean to self. While this response is natural, in perpetual practice its pending self-absorption is miserable. In some ways man's egocentrism is a secret lust for omnipotence, vying to be his own god and have all power. Our first reaction might be to deny we've ever had such a desire. Meanwhile, many of us take immediate responsibility for handling most of the problems in our midst, changing most of the people we know, and feeding our control addiction with the drug of manipulation. Simply put, we try to play God and, frankly, it's exhausting. Those of us who are redeemed are also given what 1 Corinthians 2:16 calls "the mind of Christ." Life takes on a far more accurate estimation and perspective when we learn to view it increasingly through the vantage point of the One who spoke it into existence.

List in the margin three or four of your greatest challenges or concerns.

Now go back and write the words *before the throne* before each of those challenges. The heart of prayer is moving those very kinds of challenges from the insecurities and uncertainties of earth to the throne of God. Only then can they be viewed with dependable accuracy and

Then I saw a Lamb, looking as if it had been slain, standing in the center of the throne, encircled by the four living creatures and the elders. —Revelation 5:6

You are worthy, our Lord and God, to receive glory and honor and power, for you created all things, and by your will they were created and have their being.
—Revelation 4:11

boundless hope. Go back to your original drawing of the elements in the throne room of God. Insert every one of the challenges you mentioned earlier into that diagram. In other words, write the phrases in the depiction. Look carefully at the drawing; then close your eyes and do your best to picture the glorious seraphim never ceasing to cry "Holy, holy, holy!" Imagine the lightning emitting from the throne. Hear the rumblings and the thunder. Picture the elders overwhelmed by God's worthiness, casting their crowns before the throne. I ask you the following question under my own tremendous personal conviction: Do we think the God, the blessed and only Ruler, the King of kings and Lord of lords, who alone is immortal and who lives in unapproachable light, can manage our lives and our problems? Oh, Beloved, fight the good fight of faith! Approach the throne of grace with confidence! Your God is huge.

KEY SCRIPTURE

GREAT AND MARVELOUS ARE YOUR DEEDS, LORD GOD ALMIGHTY. JUST AND TRUE ARE YOUR WAYS, KING OF THE AGES. WHO WILL NOT FEAR YOU, O LORD, AND BRING GLORY TO YOUR NAME? FOR YOU ALONE ARE HOLY. ALL NATIONS WILL COME AND WORSHIP BEFORE YOU, FOR YOUR RIGHTEOUS ACTS HAVE BEEN REVEALED.
—REVELATION 15:3-4

The Lord is not slow in keeping his promise, as some understand slowness. He is patient with you, not wanting anyone to perish, but everyone to come to repentance.
—2 Peter 3:9

🌴 The Wrath of God 🌴

Unfortunately, we cannot claim to be serious students about what John seemed to want us to know most yet avoid the subject of God's prophesied wrath in the Book of Revelation. If Revelation were a movie and the images we'll study today came on the screen, I would undoubtedly head for a refill of popcorn. However, Revelation is no movie. And opposed to its popularity in the fiction genre, it's also non-fiction. I'm not glad. Perhaps the truest words that ever fall from tainted human lips are these: God is faithful. Indeed He is. What may trouble us today is that He is always faithful. In other words, God always does what He insists He will whether we like it or not. The idealist in me wishes the wrath of God didn't even exist and would never be unleashed. Then the realist in me …

- Reads accounts of unspeakable cruelties and abuses to children,
- Hears the name of God mocked and profaned publicly through media,
- Listens to the arrogant who have convinced themselves they are gods, and
- Sees the violence bred by hatred, ignorance, and prejudice.

Then like most of you, I look around me, shudder with horror, and think, "Where is the fear of God?"

Not Wanting Any to Perish

At times in my life I've looked no further than my own mirror or my own church and wondered the words of Lamentations 3:22, "Because of the Lord's great love we are not consumed." I have said to Him more times than I can count, "Lord, why You do not rend this earth and swallow up Your own people, not to mention this godless world, is beyond me." Of course, the reason He spares believers is because He did not spare His own Son. (See Rom. 8:32.) Why does He continue to put up with a world that increasingly mocks Him? Why does He wait? For all of time, the most succinct answer to those questions can be found in 2 Peter 3:9.

Praise God His Word never changes. Before we turn our attentions to several chapters in Revelation, I'd like for you to read the context of the verse you just noted.

Read 2 Peter 3:1-15. Write three facts from this 15-verse segment.

The Coming Wrath

In some ways the wrath of God will simply finish off what man has started. I am convinced that mankind will do a proficient job of nearly destroying himself and his own planet based on the wars and conflicts prophesied in the Book of Daniel concerning the end of time. God's Word promises a new heaven and a new earth but not until this one is destroyed. Matthew 24 prophesies increasing wickedness and destruction toward the end of time, with a mounting strength and frequency of birth pains (vv. 4-8). Toward the very end of this age, God will allow the full measure of all permissible wrath to be poured out upon this earth: the wrath of man (never under-estimate it), the unholy wrath of Satan, and the holy wrath of God. No wonder this time of great tribulation will be like no other. The wrath described in the Book of Revelation unfolds in a somewhat mysterious sequence that Scripture tags Seals, Trumpets, and Bowls.

Read the segments regarding each one and note one description that stands out most to you. You will notice that the Seals introduce the Trumpets and the Trumpets usher in the Bowls.

The Seals: Revelation 6:1-17; 8:1-5

The Trumpets: Revelation 8:6-13; 9:1-21

The Bowls: Revelation 16

Unsettling is an understatement. My horror is primarily for those who refuse to believe. In your own words, what does God's Word say to believers in 1 Thessalonians 1:9-10?

Saved from Wrath

I am not implying that believers won't go through terrible times. The Word is clear we will (2 Tim. 3:1-5), and in many ways and in countless countries Christians already are. My point is that the wrath of God described in the Book of Revelation is not toward the redeemed. They will either be delivered from it or through it. The inoculation against the coming wrath of God is confessing His Son as Savior and repenting of sin. No one who comes to Him with a sincere heart of reception and repentance will be refused … unless they wait too late.

God will reveal Himself in countless ways toward the end of time, pouring out His Spirit, His wonders, and His mercies. Those mercies, however, are bestowed according to demand. In other words, some people respond to tender mercies. Others don't respond until God shows severe mercies. Others don't respond at all. Never forget that God wants to save people. Not destroy them. During the last days, the heavens will show so many signs and evangelists will preach so powerfully that I am convinced people will practically have to work at refusing Him. Yet many tragically will.

Why will people refuse to believe, according to Romans 2:5?

REFLECTION

MANY PEOPLE STRUGGLE WITH GOD'S WRATH. THINK ABOUT YOUR OWN PICTURE OF GOD. DO YOU SEE GOD AS A GOD WHO ACTS IN JUDGMENT AT APPROPRIATE TIMES? DO YOU NEED A GREATER UNDERSTANDING OF GOD?

They tell how you turned to God from idols to serve the living and true God, and to wait for his Son from heaven, whom he raised from the dead—Jesus, who rescues us from the coming wrath.
—1 Thessalonians 1:9-10

Because of your stubbornness and your unrepentant heart, you are storing up wrath against yourself for the day of God's wrath, when his righteous judgment will be revealed.—Romans 2:5

God Always Acts According to His Character

Beloved, please hear my heart. The wrath of God cannot be dissected from the character and Person of God. In other words, even in His unleashed wrath, God cannot be less than who He is. God is holy. He is good. He is love. God is righteous and God is right. The Judge will judge; but unlike our judgments, His judgments are always based on truth. (Glance at Rom. 2:2.)

Ours is also a God of inconceivable compassion, forgiveness, and mercy. I need look no further than the hands on this keyboard for proof. How He has forgiven me! When others might have left me for dead and said I got what I deserved, He tended my filthy, self-inflicted wounds and pulled me from the ditch.

God is neither mean nor unjust. He is Holy. Beloved, God will judge this world. The Day of the Lord will come, and none will doubt He is God. He will not be mocked. He'd have to be untrue to His own character to do otherwise. Conclude by reading Revelation 15:1-5.

I love the reference to the song of Moses and the song of the Lamb. You see, God will bring inconceivable order and completion out of a season that will seem the ultimate chaos and destruction. The end of time will see the culmination of the brilliant plan of God rising like a resurrected life from the smoldering tomb of earth. From the back this resurrected life looks like the old covenant. From the front, He looks like the new covenant. But when all is said and done, the two will be seen as they were always intended: as one perfect whole. As one perfect life: Christ's. And all will make sense.

KEY SCRIPTURE

AND THE DEVIL, WHO DECEIVED THEM, WAS THROWN INTO THE LAKE OF BURNING SULFUR, WHERE THE BEAST AND THE FALSE PROPHET HAD BEEN THROWN. THEY WILL BE TORMENTED DAY AND NIGHT FOR EVER AND EVER.
—REVELATION 20:10

✹ The Devil's Doom ✹

Few words characterize the end of time better than *intense*. All things—both good and evil—intensify like the crescendo of a trumpet hailing the King of kings and a government with no end. We cannot comprehend the ways and means by which God will work out "everything in conformity with the purpose of His will" (Eph. 1:11), but we can trust an all-wise sovereign and supreme God who can do no wrong. When I read Daniel 4:37, I insert my name rather than Nebuchadnezzar's; and I read it aloud over my own life. Write your own name in the margin; then read the verse aloud.

The Kings of the Earth

Read Revelation 19:11-21. Astonishing as it is, masses of people will still gather with the beast to make war against the rider on the horse and His army. After unprecedented signs and wonders and mercies of God ranging from tender to severe, many will refuse to repent. They will exercise the foolish audacity to stand as a foe against the blazing Son of God. Why? I believe one primary reason exceeds all others when God is rejected in the face of overwhelming evidence in His favor: unwillingness to bow to authority.

Notice the wording in Revelation 19:19 and fill in the blank.

Based on glorious Scriptures like Revelation 7:9, we know that innumerable peoples will turn to Jesus Christ and be saved in the last days. Revelation 19 and 20 also tell us that many will perish in their arrogant refusal to turn to Truth. I can't help but focus on the reference to the "kings of the earth." The Word intimates that some of those who refuse to bow will be the reputed power brokers of the earth. Their lust for dominance will literally be the death of them, and how foolish! In their refusal to bow to a righteous God, they will bow to the prince of hell. Satan's scheme is as old as his first appearance in the garden. He tries to convince us that we can be our own bosses. Our own gods. But we were fashioned to serve under a greater rule. Man has no sovereign authority. We cannot be our own bosses no matter how we deny our purpose.

Exactly how will Christ strike down His foes according to Revelation 19:15,21?

The Sword of His Mouth

I believe a sword symbolizes Christ's tongue, because He will strike down His foes by the words of His mouth. His is the same mouth that spoke the universe into existence and whirled the earth into orbit. How fitting that God assigned John the Revelator the privilege of announcing Christ's returning title as stated in Revelation 19:13.

What is it? _____

No other inspired writer was given the insight into the *Logos* (Jesus Christ). The same Word made flesh to dwell among us will also return with the shout of victory as His foes fall at His feet. Every knee will bow … one way or the other.

Satan Chained

Read Revelation 20:1-6. I am immediately struck by the irony that references to a "great chain" and being "set free" are found right here in passages prophesying the devil's future. Scripture tells us that Satan will be bound for a thousand years before he is thrown into the lake of burning sulfur. (See Rev. 20:10.) Scholars are very divided over whether or not the time reference is literal. I tend to prefer the principle that purports: when plain sense makes common sense, seek no other sense. I have no trouble picturing a literal millennium. At the same time, I am certainly no scholar; and I also recognize 2 Peter 3:8.

I see one fact as undeniable in Revelation 20:2. No matter the time frame, Satan will be bound for a season. I couldn't be happier that the means is a great chain. How appropriate! Some may wonder why God will bother chaining him for a time rather than simply casting him immediately into the lake of fire. Beloved, as far as I'm concerned, the last days will be high time for Satan to be bound in chains! Perhaps it is for all of us who have cried, "How long, O sovereign Lord, until You avenge our bondage?" I can't wait for Satan to know how chains feel. In fact, I hope the "great chain" is made from all the ones that have fallen off our ankles!

Released for a Time

Revelation 20:3 offers what may be the ultimate irony. After a season of bondage, Satan will be "set free" by God for "a short time." Of course, this "freedom" will not be liberty from sin and rebellion but freedom to once again rise up in rebellion against God.

Read Revelation 20:7-10. I suppose we need not worry about whether Satan will learn his lesson while chained in the abyss. He is the embodiment of evil. He will return to his old tricks the moment he is released, exceedingly empowered by ever-increasing rage.

John 8:44 provides a succinct synopses of Satan. How is he characterized?

When Satan is released upon the masses once more, he will come speaking his native language. His is so effectively deceptive that if undefended, he can delude the brightest then delight in the cycle he spun. Make no mistake about it: deceived people deceive people. If you have ever dealt with a deeply deceived and deceiving person, you know that the only defense is prayer. Rationalizing is useless. Only God Himself can break the cycle of deception.

The Final Rebellion

In the final rebellion, masses of people will choose to stand in defiance against the holy Son of God. Mind you, by this time Christ will be fully revealed. We can only imagine what schemes of deception the evil one will use to convince them that he can promise them more than God their Maker. My guess is that they will be deluded into thinking that they are choosing their own lusts and greeds rather than an eternity of holiness in the presence of God. They will know the truth yet they will choose a lie. Thinking they are choosing themselves, they will choose the devil. Hell will be eternal bondage to torment. I cannot bear the thought of it and want no one to go there. Let's take a look at the last segment of Scripture in today's lesson.

The Judgment

Read Revelation 20:11-15. In this passage, we see a picture of God seated in judgment. To stand before the great white throne will indeed be a terrifying experience for those without Christ. Those who know Christ have no reason to fear judgment. Their names will be found in the book of life. For believers, there will be no condemnation. (See Rom. 8:1.) Those outside of Christ, however, will face the lake of fire. They will have no place to run from God.

Look carefully at Revelation 20:13. How will each person who stands before the great white throne be judged?

God began His magnificent creation of humankind with one man. Though planet earth now bulges with six billion people, God still breathes life into each being one at a time. We were fashioned for God and designed to seek Him. He created a universe and an order with the divine purpose of bearing constant witness to His existence. Heaven unceasingly declares His glory and all who truly seek Him find Him.

The New Jerusalem

Today our thoughts will center on the sights John beheld in Revelation 21. Look only at the first word of Revelation 21:1. *Then.* Oh, Beloved, how I thank God for *then*. Your life may be difficult right now. Your challenges may be more than you can stand. Your health may be terrible. No matter how difficult this present season, Dear One, God has a *then* on your timeline of faith. Every believer has a new chapter ahead filled with dreams come true. Whatever you are facing is not the end of the story. Read all of Revelation 21, continually contrasting its hopes with the horrors of the chapter preceding it.

According to Revelation 21:1, what was different in the new heavens and the new earth? Fill in the blank in the margin.

The End of Separation

I long for the day when seas will no longer separate brothers and sisters in the family of God. I want to know my faithful brothers in Sudan, Iran, and all over the world. Remember, much of the terminology in the final book of the Bible is figurative. I believe the reference in Revelation 21:1 to "no longer any sea" means that nothing else will ever separate us. We will be one just as Christ asked the Father. We will have all the beauty of the oceans without their forbiddings.

The Holy City

After telling us the new heavens and earth will not be separated by seas, John depleted no little ink describing the new Jerusalem. Meditate on his words, "I saw the Holy City" (v. 2). I am convinced that most Gentiles like me cannot relate to the attachment many Jews through the centuries have felt toward their homeland. Even those whose feet never touched the holy land yearned for it like a lost child longs for his mother.

I saw this peculiar bond just weeks ago in the face of Arie, my Hebrew friend and ancient lands guide. He and his family are now residents of Tel Aviv, but his heart never departs Jerusalem. The turmoil erupting within and around Jerusalem doesn't just concern or upset him. It brings him pain. I asked him how he felt about the ongoing crises in the holy land; as I witnessed the agony in his face, I sorrowed that I had asked something so obviously intimate.

How would you describe the attachment of many Jews through the ages according to Psalm 137:5-6?

Arie told me that the deeply heartfelt commitment to keep Jerusalem ever before them is restated at every orthodox Jewish wedding. In the midst of joy, they always "remember" Jerusalem and the tragic loss of the Temple. If Arie and other Jews through the ages have experienced an indescribable attachment to the holy city and a sense of grief concerning the temple, try to imagine the strength of John's ties. He grew up on the shores of Galilee at the highest peak of Jerusalem's splendor since the days of Solomon's temple. Herod's temple was one of the greatest wonders of John's world. No Jew could behold her splendor without marveling.

KEY SCRIPTURE

I SAW THE HOLY CITY, THE NEW JERUSALEM, COMING DOWN OUT OF HEAVEN FROM GOD, PREPARED AS A BRIDE BEAUTIFULLY DRESSED FOR HER HUSBAND.
—REVELATION 21:2

"There was no longer any
_____."—Revelation 21:1

If I forget you, O Jerusalem, may my right hand forget its skill. May my tongue cling to the roof of my mouth if I do not remember you, if I do not consider Jerusalem my highest joy.—Psalm 137:5-6

John knew every wall and gate of the holy city. He walked her lengths and breadths with the Savior Himself. He sat not far from Him on the Mount of Olives overlooking her beauty. John was also part of the generation who saw her total destruction in A.D. 70. By the time she fell, John probably was already stationed in Ephesus; but the news traveled fast, and the sobs echoed louder with every mile.

Then John "saw the Holy city, the new Jerusalem, coming down out of heaven from God, prepared as a bride beautifully dressed for her husband." How his heart must have leapt with unspeakable joy! There she was! Not just restored but created anew with splendor beyond compare. I wonder if John was weeping at the sight. I cannot imagine seeing my Christ and my God and their heavenly Kingdom and not weeping. Our last tears, however, will no longer be those shed in mourning, for …

"There will be no more death or mourning or crying or pain, for the _____ _____ of things has passed away" (Rev. 21:4).

The New Order

Ever since Adam and Eve grieved the loss of intimate fellowship with God and the agony of one son murdered by the other, this present earth has been characterized by the "old order." We are shocked by pain again and again, yet this present world order is literally characterized by it. None of us will avoid the pain. We can anesthetize the pain, but we will not fully celebrate the new order without it.

What part of this "old order" will you be happiest to bid farewell?

The new order will bring all things to completion and prepare the heavens and the earth for eternal bliss. "Now the dwelling of God is with men." Hallelujah! The sorrow of man's expulsion from the garden will only be exceeded by the unquenchable joy of the dwelling of God with men. You may have noticed that John did not see a temple in this new Jerusalem, nor did he see a sun or a moon.

Why will these elements be absent in the new holy city according to Revelation 21:22-23?

The Kings of the New Earth

Did you notice another reference to "the kings of the earth" in verse 24? These kings stand in stark contrast to the kings of the earth in Revelation 19:19 who will rise against the rider called Faithful and True. I believe the "kings of the earth" who will bring splendor into the new holy city may be the redeemed described in Revelation 20:4 and others like them.

When God creates the new heaven and the new earth, I think quite possibly those who reign with Him in the Kingdom—not as equals but as those ruling under His authority—will be among those bringing "their splendor into" the new holy city. I also believe that prior to the end of time, kings of many nations will bow their knees in adoration and confession of Jesus

Christ, the Son of God. Indeed, "the glory and honor of the nations will be brought into it." Our future is beyond the words and imaginations of scholars, poets, and Spielbergs. We will bask in the brilliance of our God when He proclaims a new beginning and creates a heaven and an earth out of the ideal of His imagination.

According to Revelation 21:14, what did John see on the 12 foundations of the city wall?

The Twelve Apostles

Beloved, do you realize that among the 12 foundations John saw his own name? In the days he remained on this earth, can you imagine what kinds of thoughts he must have had as he recaptured that sight in his memory? I have no idea what being one of Jesus' disciples was like, but I don't think that they felt superhuman or vaguely worthy of their calling. I'm not even sure those original disciples ever grasped that what they were doing would have a mammoth effect. I can't picture them thinking, "What I'm doing this moment will go down in history and be recorded in the eternal annals of glory." I think they probably got down on themselves just like you and I do. I also think they were terribly overwhelmed at the prospect of reaching their world with the gospel of Christ and seeing only handfuls of converts most of the time.

Can't you imagine that days and months later when John "stared" at that wall and its foundations again in his memory, he was nearly overcome that God esteemed the disciples? Don't you think that he marveled that the plan had worked … considering the mortal agents God had chosen to use? Every day of my life I deal with a measure of low self-esteem in ministry. I never feel "up to" the task. Never smart enough. Never strong enough. Never prayed up enough. Never prepared enough. Do you feel the same way? Then perhaps you also feel the same flood of emotions when this truth washes over you: God loves man. He prepares an inconceivable place for those who receive His love and highly esteems those who choose to believe His call over the paralyzing screams of their own insecurities. No, our names won't be written on the foundations of the new Jerusalem, but they are engraved in the palms of His hands.

➤ Seeing His Face ➤

We've come to a fork in the road; but before we say goodbye, let's sit down for a little while and open our Bibles together again. We happen to be reading about a river today. Why don't we go sit on a rock on its bank, take off our sandals, and put our feet in its lapping tide?

Read the last chapter in the inspired Word of God, Revelation 22, and write pertinent information in the following categories.

Additional Descriptions of the New Heaven and Earth	John's Personal Responses	Warnings	Invitations

KEY SCRIPTURE

THEY WILL SEE HIS FACE, AND HIS NAME WILL BE ON THEIR FOREHEADS. —REVELATION 22:4

Side by Side with Angels

Twice toward the end of the Revelation our protagonist became so overwhelmed at the sight of such glorious visions that he fell at the feet of the angel. (See Rev. 19:10; 22:8.) Both times John received a swift rebuke and a reminder that the angel was nothing more than a "fellow servant." Amazing, isn't it? Those who serve God virtually work side by side with the angels from glory. They are our fellow servants! Remember that next time you feel alone in your task.

I'd also like to draw another application from John's untimely buckling of the knees. John did not make the mistake of falling down at the feet of the angel when the visions were difficult and frightening to behold. He fell over the good news. Warning: Satan's primary objective is to entice us to bow to anything and anyone other than God.

Stay by the River

During our stay on this earth, our lives are meant to be like trees of life bringing forth fruit in our seasons so others can taste and see that the Lord is good. (See Ps. 34:8.) In order to bear much fruit, we've got to stay by the river. Perhaps even in it!

Turning around, Jesus saw them following and asked, "What do you want?" —John 1:38

The river in both visions seems to represent the outpouring of God's power and anointing. As we conclude our present journey together, I pray we've progressed in our walk with God, taken off our rationalizing seat belts, and thrown ourselves into His great adventure. If you've taken part in our sessions, you will remember that in the introduction we considered the first words of Christ penned by the apostle John. They came in the form of a question. (See John 1:38.)

Based on Ezekiel 47:3-6, how deeply do you see yourself in the figurative "river" of His power and activity? In other words, how deeply have you involved yourself with Christ?

__ **Still on the bank**   __ **Ankle-deep**   __ **Knee-deep**   __ **Waist-deep**   __ **Swimming**

Reflect on where you were when we began this journey. Beloved, I don't want you to be discouraged if you're not waist-deep or swimming. I am asking only if you and I are more deeply immersed in Christ than when we began. Are we progressing? That's one of the most important questions of all. Mind you, we can swim one season and crawl our way right back to the bank the next. We will not be completely "healed" of our inconsistencies, infirmities, and weaknesses until we see Christ face-to-face.

They Will See His Face

Face-to-face. I hope you didn't miss the most beautiful statement in the final chapter of Scripture. "They will see His face …" For many of us, the very sight of His face will be heaven enough. Everything else is the River overflowing its banks. Until then, we who are redeemed are wrapped in prison walls of flesh. Our view is impaired by the steel bars of mortal vision. We are not unlike Moses who experienced God's presence but could not see His face. To him and to all confined momentarily by mortality, God has said, "You cannot see my face, for no one may see me and live" (Ex. 33:20).

When all is said and done, we who are alive in Christ will indeed see His face and live. Happily ever after. I can hardly wait; yet right this moment I am absorbed by the thought of someone else seeing that face. Several of the early church fathers plant the apostle John back in the soil of Ephesus again after the conclusion of his exile on the Island of Patmos.

John ended his life a true friend of Christ, for he took on His interests as surely as Elisha took on the cloak of Elijah. Early church fathers reported that long after John lacked the strength to walk, the Beloved Disciple was carried in a chair through crowds gathered for worship. His final sermons were short and sweet. "My little children, love one another!" He poured his life into love. Christ's love. The focus of his final days captures the two concepts I've learned above all others in this eight-week journey:

• Christ calls His beloved disciples to forsake ambition for affection. John moved from his "pillar" position in the Jerusalem church to relative obscurity. It's better to pour out our lives in places unknown than to become dry bones in the places we've always been.

• Only disciples who are convinced they are "beloved" will in turn love beyond themselves. Actively embracing the lavish love of God is our only means of extending divine love to injured hearts. We simply cannot give what we do not have.

Our Abba seems to have made a practice of telling us almost nothing about the actual deaths of His saints. All we know according to Psalm 116:15 is that their deaths were precious to Him. In fact, we might surmise that the exclusion of details is precisely because they were so precious to Him. Intimate. And none of our business. But don't think for a moment the Savior wasn't nearby when the sounds of an old Son of Thunder grew faint … then silent. After all, John was among the very few who stood nearby when the Incarnate Word fell silent.

John's death would mark the close of the most critical era of human history. He was the single remaining apostle who could make the claims of his own pen.

At his age, John's fragile body probably showed symptoms of failing some hours or even days before he breathed his last. If loved ones were gathered around him, they likely did what most of us would do. They tried to make him as comfortable as possible. They may have gently slipped a pillow of sorts under his head to help support him as his lungs heaved for air. That's what we did when my mother's fragile frame could no longer sustain the strength to house her soul.

I'm not sure John needed a pillow however. Somehow I picture him in his death much like he had been in his life. To me, the scene that captures the Beloved Disciple most is recorded in John 13:23 at a certain table decades earlier. The Amplified Version says it best. "One of His disciples whom Jesus loved—whom He esteemed and delighted in—was reclining [next to Him] on Jesus' bosom."[2] Yes, perhaps John died just as he lived. Nestled close. Reclining on the breast of an unseen but very present Savior, John's weary head in His tender arms. The Spirit and the bride said, "Come!" And in the distance could be heard a gentle thunder.

1. From *Hebrew Greek Key Word Study Bible* © 1996 AMG International, Inc.
2. From *The Amplified New Testament* © The Lockman Foundation 1954, 1958, 1987. Used by permission.

Precious in the sight of the Lord is the death of his saints.
—Psalm 116:15

That which was from the beginning, which we have heard, which we have seen with our eyes, which we have looked at and our hands have touched—this we proclaim concerning the Word of life. —1 John 1:1

REFLECTION

HOW ARE YOU LIVING THE ESSENCE OF JOHN 15:12-17?

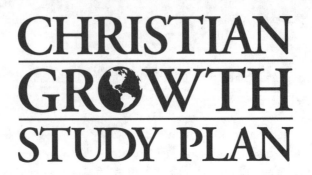

CHRISTIAN GROWTH STUDY PLAN

In the **Christian Growth Study Plan (formerly Church Study Course),** this book *John: The Beloved Disciple, Student Edition* is a resource for course credit in the subject area "Personal Life" of the Christian Growth category of plans. To receive credit, read the book, complete the learning activities, show your work to your pastor, a staff member or church leader, then complete the following information. This page may be duplicated. Send the completed page to:

Christian Growth Study Plan
One LifeWay Plaza
Nashville, TN 37234-0117
FAX: (615)251-5067
Email: cgspnet@lifeway.com

For information about the Christian Growth Study Plan, refer to the Christian Growth Study Plan Catalog. It is located online at www.lifeway.com/cgsp. If you do not have access to the Internet, contact the Christian Growth Study Plan office (1.800.968.5519) for the specific plan you need for your ministry.

John: The Beloved Disciple, Student Edition
COURSE NUMBER: CG-0724

PARTICIPANT INFORMATION

Rev. 5-02

Social Security Number (USA Only-optional) | Personal CGSP Number* | Date of Birth (Mo., Day, Yr.)

Name (First, MI, Last) | Home Phone

Address (Street, Route, or P.O. Box) | City, State, or Province | Zip/Postal Code

CHURCH INFORMATION

Church Name

Address (Street, Route, or P.O. Box) | City, State, or Province | Zip/Postal Code

CHANGE REQUEST ONLY

❑Former Name

❑Former Address | City, State, or Province | Zip/Postal Code

❑Former Church | City, State, or Province | Zip/Postal Code

Signature of Pastor, Conference Leader, or Other Church Leader | Date

*New participants are requested but not required to give SS# and date of birth. Existing participants, please give CGSP# when using SS# for the first time. Thereafter, only one ID# is required. *Mail To:* Christian Growth Study Plan, One LifeWay Plaza, Nashville, TN 37234-0117. Fax: (615)251-5067.